THE
ENERGY
SECRET

THE
ENERGY
SECRET

Practices and Rituals to Unlock Your
Inner Energy for Healing & Happiness

JANE ALEXANDER

Illustrations by
AMALIA WAHLSTRÖM

STERLING ETHOS
New York

For James—
simply the best energy secret

STERLING ETHOS
New York

An Imprint of Sterling Publishing Co., Inc.
1166 Avenue of the Americas
New York, NY 10036

Text © 2020 Jane Alexander
Illustrations © 2020 Amalia Wahlström

ISBN 978-1-4549-4079-1

Distributed in Canada by Sterling Publishing Co., Inc.
c/o Canadian Manda Group, 664 Annette Street
Toronto, Ontario M6S 2C8, Canada

For information about custom editions, special sales, and premium and corporate purchases, please
contact Sterling Special Sales at 800-805-5489 or specialsales@sterlingpublishing.com.

Manufactured in Malaysia

2 4 6 8 10 9 7 5 3 1

sterlingpublishing.com

Design by Nicky Collings

CONTENTS

8   INTRODUCTION

What is energy?

PART ONE | BODY ENERGY

14   1   FEELING THE ENERGY IN YOUR BODY

Get in touch with your body | Paying attention exercise | Bone-balancing | Heart searching | Your other organs | Breathing—a direct route to energy-working | The complete breath | The breath of fire | Therapeutic breathwork

27   2   AURAS AND CHAKRAS

How to start seeing auras | Seeing someone else's aura | Seeing your own aura | Balance your chakras for health and harmony | Getting in touch with chakra energy | Looking at the chakras | The base chakra | The sacral chakra | The solar plexus chakra | The heart chakra | The throat chakra | The brow chakra | The crown chakra | Contacting the chakras through sound

40   3   HEALING THERAPIES FOR THE BODY

Shiatsu—finger pressure for simple healing | First steps in shiatsu | Banishing headaches | Soothing insomnia | Banishing the blues—boosting energy | Healing | Awakening your hands | Channeling healing energy | Healing someone else | Energy games | Taking healing further | Flower essences | The Bach flower remedies | For fear | For uncertainty | For loneliness | For oversensitivity | For despondency or despair | For overconcern for others | For insufficient interest in the present | Sound therapy | Color therapy | Color breathing | Color correspondences

60   4   THE ENERGETIC POWER OF FOOD

Spirit and soul food | Creating food with loving energy | Soul shopping and spiritual cookery | Make mealtimes special

68 **5** ENERGY EXERCISE

Exercise as meditation | Ancient exercises tailor-made for today | The starting posture | Turning the head and twisting the tail | Dragon stamping | Yoga—mobilizing energy | Which yoga would suit me? | You're an absolute beginner | You want something clear and precise | You want something holistic | You get easily bored | You want something strong but spiritual | You are totally exhausted | The energy of the dance | Biodanza | Home dance class

PART TWO | EMOTIONAL ENERGY

84 **6** WORKING WITH EMOTIONAL ENERGY

Tracking unwanted emotional energy | Keep a journal—record your dreams | Liberating emotional energy | Your energy cleansers | Dealing with other people's energy | Shielding techniques | Guardians and allies | Creating energetic rapport | Solo exercise | Joint exercise

100 **7** SEXUAL ENERGY

Introducing Tantra | Bringing sacred sexuality into everyday life | Cultivating sensuality | Playing with sensual energy | Connecting with the breath | The seesaw | Back bends | Sensual massage | Sacred sexuality | Animal sexuality | Uncovering the wild within | Elemental sex | Raising energy with Tantra

PART THREE | ENVIRONMENTAL ENERGY

114 **8** THE ENERGY OF THE HOME

Sensing the energy of your home | Decluttering and cleansing | Clearing techniques | Clapping | Sage cleansing | Incense | Sound cleansing | Feng shui and vastu shastra | Simple home energizers and harmonizers | Use air purifiers | Name your space | Use the power of scent | Allow sound into your home | Have life in your house | Choose well-crafted products | Fill your home with flowers | Bringing color into your home | Balancing the energy of your home with the elements | Fire—the energizer | Water—the purifier | Air—the transformer | Earth—the strengthener

126 9 NATURAL ENERGY

Reconnecting with earth energy | Stone and leaf energy | Listening to earth energy |
The shamanic path | The medicine path | Sacred energy | Seasonal energy

138 10 CITIES AND THE WORKPLACE

City energy | Space dancing | Energy commuting | City medicine |
Conscious manifestation | Office energy | The office sanctuary
Office magic | Energetic meetings

PART FOUR | SPIRITUAL ENERGY

150 11 CONNECTING TO SPIRITUAL ENERGY

The Kabbalah—a map of energy | The Tree of Life | Malkuth—the kingdom
| Yesod—the foundation | Hod—glory | Netzach—victory | Tiphareth—beauty |
Geburah—severity | Chesed—mercy (sometimes known as love) | Daath—knowledge
| Binah—understanding | Chockmah—wisdom | Kether—the crown | Building the
inner temple | Building your inner temple | The temple of Malkuth |
Journeying | Freeform journeying | Guided journeying |
Bringing spiritual energy into your cells

166 12 HONORING DARK ENERGY

Seeking our shadow | Shadow-working | The "other chair" technique | Paint your
shadow | Write to your shadow figure | Plumbing the depths | The descent of Innana

178 13 DEATH—THE END OF ENERGY?

Deathworking | A year to live | Where were you before you were born? | The dark path
| Claiming our energetic heritage

188 INDEX

192

     ACKNOWLEDGMENTS

INTRODUCTION

---- ✳ ----

WHAT IS ENERGY?

What links sex and shiatsu? What connects feng shui to cooking? What does a business meeting share with a yoga class or a swim in the sea? The answer lies in one simple word—energy. Vital energy runs through all of life. It connects our bodies to our minds, our emotions, and our souls. It links us to other people, our homes, nature, and the wider world; it connects us to the universe and the highest spiritual power.

We cannot see this subtle yet powerful force—but it affects every moment of our being. When our vital energy becomes sluggish, life seems dull or difficult: we start to move through each day as if through treacle—and there is no joy, no dreaming, no fun. Relationships become sticky, bodies feel under par, work is a chore, and home never feels quite right. At the other extreme, if energy is running out of control, life becomes a roller-coaster: we feel constantly stressed and strained, our nerves jangle; we start to exist in a melée of arguments and irritability.

Once we start to recognize how our energy flows and work with it, everything changes. Life takes on fresh meaning and purpose. We enjoy a sense of ease in our bodies. Our relationships with partners, friends, family, and workmates become honest, exciting, and supportive. Home transforms into a place filled with a warm, embracing atmosphere. We start to feel kinship with the whole of creation—from the urban cityscape to the wild elements of nature. Work and play intermingle to become fulfilling, exciting, and creative. Best of all, we no longer feel alone in a large, often frightening universe when we are at ease we become linked to spirit, joined to the source of all energy.

At first, the concept of energy seems rather nebulous. We talk about feeling "full" of energy, verve, enthusiasm, or pure joie de vivre. We understand the scientific concept of energy—generating power, motion, light, and movement. However, now we are beginning to become more aware of what is known as subtle or vital energy. Vital energy is the unseen force that moves through all of creation—through our bodies, our homes, the landscape, and throughout the universe. This is the energy that acupuncturists speak of as passing along meridians, the unseen pathways of the body. It is this energy that the clairvoyant sees as an aura, a cocoon of shimmering light around us. It is the energy that feng shui consultants describe as "qi" (pronounced chi) as it moves through our homes and our environment, and what the Indian mystics call "prana"—the living force, which animates our food, our bodies, and our relationships.

Choosing to live with energy is to tap into an endless source of personal power and joy. It is a lifestyle choice, the lifestyle choice for this millennium—affecting every area of daily life in the deepest possible way. As Margot Gordon, a wonderful bodywork practitioner who I know, puts it: "We're looking at the rise of "Qi Culture"—acceptance and understanding of energy will infuse all our lives in every way." I agree. In the near future, energy-working will become a familiar, accepted part of everyday life. We will think nothing of healing our bodies with energy, rather than crude medications. Ancient civilizations understood that we are not just flesh and bones; we are infused with a subtle form of energy that cannot be seen by the naked eye or under the microscope of science.

Long ago, healers from China, India, Tibet, and the Middle East developed ways of mapping the subtle energy centers and pathways of the body and applied their knowledge in precise ways to promote healing. Shamanic cultures from all around the world shift energy in their ceremonies—with often miraculous and seemingly inexplicable results. Some researchers and mystics believe that long-lost civilizations such as Atlantis, Mu, and Lemuria held the secrets of vibrational healing— turning away from surgery and drugs to use subtle energy healing methods: color, sound, flower, and gem essences.

I believe that we are on the brink of an explosion in energy medicine. I can envision a future where energy healers will scan our bodies for lack of balance and be able to correct it without the need for invasive surgery. Even better, we will be able to detect imbalance in ourselves and take steps to redress it—without the need to seek professional help.

This will become the ultimate form of preventative medicine, gently healing emotional trauma and even genetic material before it becomes pathological. We will be able to uncover and eradicate the psycho-spiritual traumas which underlie much of modern illness before they become a physiological problem.

The homes of the future will be havens of peace and joy. Through their understanding of the concepts of vital energy, our architects and builders will produce homes with true spirit and soul. Decorators will realize that the colors, textures, lights, and shapes they choose will affect not only our aesthetic sense but also our moods and feelings—they will be able to tailor your home to fit your innermost needs. Simple energy techniques will enable you to create the ambience you need in your home—whether a vibrant party place or serene sanctuary. Working with energy will allow you to guard your property and yourself, with an invisible safety fence.

Energy underpins relationships too. Just as we need smooth harmonious energy flowing through our bodies and homes, we also need to invest time in sensing and smoothing the energy between ourselves and the people we love and work with. Whether connecting with your partner, child, friend or boss, when you learn how to harmonize the energy between you, your relationships will undoubtedly improve. If all of society were to learn energy healing techniques, the world would undoubtedly be a safer, happier, and a more relaxed place.

Continuing our look into the future, I would hope that an understanding of energy might bring about more respect for our environment, for the planet. Once we all have greater understanding of how energy flows, it will become a travesty to build houses, offices, or malls in places where the earth's energy needs to flow unrestricted. You can almost feel the earth wince as we ride roughshod over its meandering energy pathways—clogging its "arteries" and "veins" with concrete and iron.

Having a sense of its vital energy could teach us where it is right to build and where to leave nature wild and free. We would recognize that this beautiful planet is our home, our only home—and we would treat it with love and respect.

At the ultimate level, cultivating energy leads to a wonderful sense of spiritual renewal. Some people have a vibrant living faith, either as part of an orthodox religion or through a private sense of belief; yet many others feel alienated from traditional religions or unable to reconcile their own feelings with the dogma and rituals of age-old sects. However, once you begin to work with energy, the outward trappings of religion become unimportant. Ultimately, it doesn't matter how you perceive God, Goddess, Creator, Great Spirit, Tao—when you connect to the living, vibrant energy of the universe, there is no need for names or titles. Instead there is a wonderful sense of belonging, of love, of peace, and connection. As beings of energy, we become united with the source of all energy and therein lies our purpose and our meaning.

The aim of this book is to introduce you to the idea of sensing, understanding and working with energy in the simplest way possible. My purpose is to get you working with energy from the very first page, so the approach is inherently practical. (If you want to read about the science, theory and philosophy of energy, there are other books which explain it very well.) Above all, I hope you find the process of energy-working fun. If at any time it becomes boring, irritating or a chore, then maybe this isn't the right time for you to be attempting this work. Leave it aside and come back to it later. We will work from the denser levels of energy in the physical body, and slowly move outward to emotional and, finally, spiritual energy. It is a wonderful journey.

Introductions over. Let's get working. Let's start feeling energy at work in our lives…

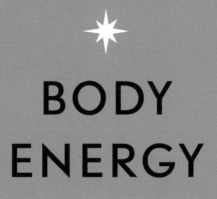

BODY
ENERGY

FEELING THE ENERGY
IN YOUR BODY

CHAPTER ONE

We will start by getting the smallest sense of the energy that flows all through our bodies. Take off your shoes and stand with your feet shoulder-length apart. Let your knees soften and allow your hands to fall gently by your sides. Imagine you have a string coming from the top of your head, right in the center of your scalp. It is attached to the ceiling and is gently tugging so you're upright but relaxed.

Close your eyes and be aware of your breath. Just stand and breathe for a few minutes. Now become aware of the center of your body, the area around your navel. Breathe deeply into that area.

How do you feel? Many people quickly start to feel a tingling through the body. It might run down your arms, radiate out from the solar plexus, or send shivers down your spine. This is your body's energy and it is reacting to this most simple exercise—you stopping for a moment to pay attention. Vital energy is always there, we just tend to ignore it. Even if you do nothing else from this book, just taking time out for two minutes a day to stand, center, and focus—and feel your energy—is a huge step. If you didn't feel the energy, don't panic. Not everyone does immediately. Just take a few minutes every so often and keep trying. It will come.

Our bodies are not just composed of flesh and blood, they are also complex chemical factories and, above all, energy powerhouses; sources of spirit. Throughout the ages, people have sought to understand the complexity of the energy systems of the body. Every great ancient culture studied the movement of energy within the human body and many charted it with great precision. Not only did they look at how much energy we have but they also studied the qualities of the energy we possess. They believed our bodies were microcosms of the universe—that what lies without in the starry cosmos also lies within, deep in the workings of the body. The Kabbalists, ancient Jewish mystics, taught that divine energy came down from the Godhead in a lightning flash, transforming itself from pure cosmic energy into matter—yet matter still infused with exactly the same spark.

Our bodies are a miracle and a profound mystery. However much we know, the remaining area of complete ignorance is still vast. Holistic physicians are convinced that the future lies not in separating body, mind and spirit, but in understanding that each is intertwined, they all affect each other. We cannot be boxed into neat compartments.

Psychoneuroimmunology explores the ways in which what we feel and think affects how our bodies work. Just as psychologists understand that our posture and body language can affect our thoughts and emotions. Bodyworkers have seen, time and time again, old memories come flooding back when they press into a muscle or connective tissue. Trauma that our ancestors experienced in previous generations can be captured in our DNA. Uplifting the soul can have miraculous effects on illness and disease. Prayer can heal. This is the work of energy within the body, the mind, and the soul. Once we learn to get in touch with that energy, we can start to experience our own lightning flash of a pure life. Let's get started…

GET IN TOUCH
WITH YOUR BODY

Most of us don't live in our bodies; we live in our heads. We can go virtually from one end of the day to the other without really thinking about our bodies. Sure, we stop for lunch—because that's our habit. Okay, we get up once in a while to go to the bathroom—our bladders are pretty hard to ignore. Yet, how often do we stop and sense our bodies? How often do we think about how they feel throughout the day? We need to become far more aware of what is actually going on at any one moment within our physical frame.

So, stop this very moment and take an inventory. Is your body stiff? Are your shoulders relaxed or up around your ears? Are you clenching your teeth so hard that your jaw is hurting? Does your body need anything? Water, perhaps? We can easily become dehydrated and tea, coffee, and fizzy drinks don't do the trick. Food? Often our bodies are just hungry for food that really sustains: a handful of nuts instead of a chocolate bar maybe; or a proper lunch of soup with sourdough bread and salad, rather than a limp supermarket sandwich. Have you been sitting so long that your back aches or your buttocks are numb? Do you need a good stretch? Do your eyes feel bright and clear, or sore and itchy? If you stare at a computer screen all day, do your eyes need to rest, or focus on something long distance for a change? Are you tired? Does your whole body need a quick catnap—or a longer rest?

Learn to listen to your body and help it any way you can. If you work at a computer, set an alarm for every thirty minutes or, at the outside, every hour. Then just quickly tune into each area of your body and see what it needs. At the very least give yourself a drink of fresh water and have a quick stretch. Get up, walk around a bit or do some simple neck rolls. If you are a busy parent or you work manually your body will be asking for different things—and most probably a rest.

Try to set aside a small amount of time every day to re-establish true meaningful contact with your body. The following exercises can help.

PAYING ATTENTION EXERCISE

Wearing loose clothes and no shoes, lay your back on the floor. Feel
where the floor supports your body. Now move your attention to your
feet—imagine the bones of your feet, the muscles, the tendons, the skin.
Are they hot or cold? Do you feel any difference between your two feet?
Are they light or heavy? Gradually work your way up your body, repeating
the questions, and becoming aware of how different parts of your body
are feeling. Move your hands up your legs and into the hips, up the torso
and into the abdomen, the chest, and the shoulders. Then down the arms
to the hands. Finish by examining your head and face.

BONE-BALANCING EXERCISE

Let's focus next on your bone structure. Using either your lightly clenched fists or the fingers of your hand, swiftly tap over your hip bones and pelvis. Listen to the sound it makes and feel the vibration in your body. Move your hands down your legs and listen and look for changes in sound and feeling. Try the soles of your feet. Work over all the bones in your body, tracking the differences.

HEART SEARCHING EXERCISE

Sit quietly and tune in to the rhythm of your heartbeat. If you feel comfortable with this (not everyone will) take your focus inside your heart, feel it pulsing. Listen to the blood sluicing through its valves. The first time I tried this exercise, I felt humbled and grateful. I was aware of (and quite overwhelmed by) its stoic power; its faithful toil. I never wanted to hurt my heart again; I wanted to give it the food and exercise it needs to function with the greatest ease. It was a turning point for me.

Sometimes "going inside" your heart can evoke feelings of panic, fear, or extreme distaste. If so, don't worry—just let the exercise go. Maybe try the exercise another time, when you could have a quite different reaction.

YOUR OTHER ORGANS

Use the same technique for getting in touch with other organs. Follow your breath into your lungs. Feel them expand and contract, pulling air into the tiny sacs. Imagine the exchange of gases, the oxygenated air flowing into all the cells. Your lungs connect you with the outside world— they are the great communicators. As you breathe in, your lungs literally inspire you: you pull in love of life, energy, enthusiasm. As you breathe out you exhale the old, the waste. Feel how your body breathes for you; it actually breathes you. You can continue this exercise to other organs. What did you discover?

If you don't feel comfortable exploring your body in this way, gently ask yourself why this is. Does it bring back any uncomfortable memories? Is it frightening? Why might this be? You might want to try this exercise every day—to see whether the feelings change. If you're just not ready for this, let the exercise go. Rest assured that, when the time is right, you'll be able to go into your body feeling fine and comfortable. You may choose to work with a therapist.

BREATHING: A DIRECT ROUTE TO ENERGY-WORKING

Once you start a relationship with your body, you will become ready to move one step further along the energy route. Breathing techniques are some of the oldest and most effective ways of awakening, stimulating, balancing, and soothing energy within the body and mind.

Breathing is a powerful medicine. The Eastern arts of yoga and qigong promise that particular forms of breathing can do everything from improving your moods or increasing your resistance to colds and illness, to fostering better sleep and even helping you resist aging. Good breathing feeds the brain, calms the nerves, and has a measurable effect on a number of medical conditions.

Some people say that how you breathe is a good indication of how you look at life altogether. Both symbolically and literally, breathing is all about taking in the new and eliminating the old. When we breathe in, we oxygenate the body through the air that we breathe and when we breathe out, we expel unwanted carbon dioxide. The Buddhist tradition regards every new breath as giving new life and every exhalation as a little death. So, taking in deep joyful breaths is seen as a way of affirming life and vitality. Breathing minimally and shallowly is like turning the volume down on the vital energy of life or accepting it, only grudgingly. There is a yoga proverb which says: "Life is in the breath. Therefore he who only half breathes, half lives."

Let's look at some simple, safe, breathing exercises that will help you become more adept at recognizing and shifting energy within your body.

THE COMPLETE BREATH

This is the basic breathing technique of pranayama, the yogic science of breathing. It is an excellent training tool as it encourages you to breathe fully, bringing oxygen deep into the cells and expelling toxins. It will also send a surge of energy through every cell of your body. Learn it lying on the floor (it's easier that way) and then you can use it whenever you need to slow down and engage your parasympathetic nervous system.

1   Lie comfortably on the floor. Bring your feet close to your buttocks and allow the knees to fall apart, bringing the soles of the feet together, hands resting gently on your abdomen. Place cushions under your knees if needed.

2   Slowly and smoothly, inhale through your nostrils, feeling your fingers parting as your abdomen expands. Many of us hold our bellies in all the time, so this may feel strange.

3   Exhale slowly and steadily through your nostrils, noticing your abdomen flatten.

4   Pause and then repeat, becoming conscious of the movement of the breath down through your chest and abdomen. Breathe at your own pace, in and out, for around five minutes.

5   If you feel comfortable, extend the breath so it comes up from the abdomen into the chest as you inhale. This provides a longer, deeper breath.

6   Finally, bring your knees together and gently stretch out your legs.

THE BREATH OF FIRE

This powerful form of yogic breathing sends the energy of your body into battle against the toxins of modern life. It strengthens the lungs, has the effect of massaging and toning the abdominal muscles, and refreshes the nervous system. However, it is strong and should not be used if you have a heart condition, high blood pressure, epilepsy, a hernia, or any ear, nose or eye problems; or if you are pregnant or menstruating.

1   This exercise can be performed sitting, standing, or lying down. Make sure you are comfortable and relaxed. Breathe regularly and normally.

2   Inhale through your nostrils slowly, smoothly and deeply—but do not strain.

3   Exhale through your nostrils briskly, as if you were sneezing. Focus your attention on your abdomen, it will automatically flatten and tighten as you exhale.

4   Allow yourself to inhale naturally—it will happen automatically following the brisk exhale.

5   Continue like this. It is energetic so don't be surprised if you only manage a minute or so to begin with.

6   Resume normal breathing and relax.

NOTE   If you are pregnant or menstruating you can use a modified form of this exercise. Instead of the "sneezing" exhale, pout your lips and allow your breath to come out in a steady stream, as if you were blowing out candles on a cake. It's a slower process but still powerful.

THERAPEUTIC BREATHWORK

During the last 50 years, new forms of breathwork have been developed. Holotropic Breathwork™ was devised by Stanislav and Christina Grof in the 1970s as a means for self-exploration and healing. Their early work used LSD (lysergic acid diethylamide) which was then a legal substance. When LSD was banned in the late sixties (the government believed it was a corrosive influence on society, thanks to its use by the counter-culture hippies), Stanislav and Grof needed a new way to continue mapping consciousness. They found that a particular form of breathing, combined with evocative music, would take people into altered states. The experience of Holotropic Breathwork is extraordinary—it can take you back to experiences from childhood, a sense of being in the womb, and even out into the starry depths of space. Rebirthing Breathwork, developed by Leonard Orr, also in the 1970s, uses a similar form of conscious connected breathing (without the music), and is used therapeutically, primarily to integrate reactions to birth trauma and to clear negative blocks.

Dr. Judith Kravitz assimilated these practices with principles from healing and spirituality to create a new hybrid technique called Transformational Breath®. Firstly, her approach teaches you how to breathe easily and effectively. Then it moves into clearing emotional blocks and trauma, and finally it opens you up to experiencing the wider dimensions of self.

More recently Stuart Sandeman has incorporated acupressure, movement, and catharsis into breathwork to create Breathpod, taking his integrated approach into the corporate world, gyms, studios, and festivals.

All of these techniques are wonderful but, as always, there are warnings— these forms of breathing can bring up painful memories. They should be used with caution and always under the supervision of a highly qualified practitioner.

AURAS
AND CHAKRAS

CHAPTER TWO

If you take time to practice the exercises from the last chapter regularly, you will become familiar with the unmistakable surge of life force as it courses through your body. By simply breathing, you will be able to feel a spark of energy tingling through you, as if you were standing beneath an exhilarating mountain waterfall. With more practice you will be able to direct this energy to particular parts of your body.

In this section, we start by looking at the aura, the cocoon of energy that vibrates around our bodies. The aura is what we recognize as a halo around the heads of spiritual beings such as Christ, Buddha, Mohammed, Vishnu, and all the prophets and angels. You don't have to be a highly evolved spiritual leader to have an aura, each and every one of us has this vibrating energy.

Auras cannot lie. The almost chemical reaction we experience when we meet someone who has an immediate and powerful impact on us (love at first sight, loathing at first sight), could be due to how our own aura reacts to someone else's. When someone feels uncomfortable in another's presence, their aura will "shrink" away from them. If someone is pushy and aggressive, their aura can envelop the other person's. On the other hand, people who feel comfortable together will show auras that happily meet or even merge into one.

HOW TO START
SEEING AURAS

---✦---

Virtually, everyone can learn how to see an aura. I trained myself by looking first at the auras of trees—they tend to be clear. Simply pick a healthy tree at some distance from you and gaze softly at it, taking your eyes slightly out of focus. You should start to see a faint shimmering of light around the tree—that's its aura. From here, you can practice on plants. How are your houseplants? Healthy or ailing? Look at the aura of a vigorous healthy plant and compare it with that of a wilted or dying plant. Next, move onto animals—see if you can detect any differences between your pets. Does your overactive puppy have a different kind of aura from your laid-back cat? Animals are very sensitive: you can give a cat an "aura stroke" by stroking about an inch or so above its fur—often the cat will start to purr as if you were physically touching it.

SEEING SOMEONE ELSE'S AURA

When you feel confident with seeing the auras of plants and animals, you can progress to people. If you have a willing subject, ask them to stand facing you, about two feet in front of a plain wall (patterns make it very hard to tell where the aura ends and the pattern begins.) Position yourself a fair distance away—ten feet is ideal. Focus on the wall behind him or her, with your eyes slightly unfocused. You should start to see a band of fuzzy light around the person.

Practice on the train, waiting in a queue, sitting in a restaurant, or when waiting for a friend. After a while you should start to notice differences between auras—some might seem brighter, others more dingy or muddy. You might notice particular colors or flashes of color.

SEEING YOUR OWN AURA

You can also train yourself to check out your own aura. Stand in front of a mirror, several feet away. Again, try to have a plain wall about two feet behind you (you could always hang up a sheet). Breathe calmly and focus on the wall, rather than yourself, softly unfocusing your eyes. Look for colors in the aura. If you can't "see" any colors, do you get any feelings about what colors might be there? Generally speaking, a colorful, clean, and bright aura shows someone who is happy and healthy. Dirty, dark colors tend to suggest either physical illness, tiredness, or some kind of emotional black cloud. Experts say that the odd flash of color in an aura could indicate an emotion that is not under control.

BALANCE YOUR CHAKRAS
FOR HEALTH AND HARMONY

✳

Eastern religions teach us that the human body contains numerous spinning spheres of bioenergetic energy, known as chakras. The seven major chakras run in a direct line from the base of the spine to the crown of the head.

The chakras are precise monitors of our physical and mental well-being. Each is said to spin at a different frequency. When each chakra spins at its perfect frequency, our emotions are balanced and we enjoy optimum health and a deep sense of peace. It's a little like tuning into a radio station: if you're on the wrong frequency, the sound becomes distorted and unpleasant; once you hit the right frequency, it becomes clear as a bell. Each chakra governs specific parts of the body and specific emotions. Once you have worked out which chakras are unbalanced, you can rectify the balance and bring them back into harmony.

GETTING IN TOUCH
WITH CHAKRA ENERGY

✳

Often, we live either with our heads in the clouds, connected to the sky, or rooted to the Earth, with our feet so stolidly in the mud that we cannot raise our eyes to the stars. In an ideal world, we achieve a balance and stand firmly on the Earth but also take inspiration from the sky. This exercise will help you to feel grounded and secure.

1   Stand comfortably with your feet shoulder-width apart, as you did in the opening exercise. Once again, imagine you have a string attached from the top of your head to the sky above, gently tugging you upright. Let your knees, pelvis, and shoulders relax. Check your jaw to make sure you are not holding any tension there.

2   Gently close your eyes and become aware of your breathing. Don't try to force it. Notice whether it automatically starts to slow down.

3   Visualize a shimmering ball of pure violet energy above your head. Breathe into this sphere, slowly and steadily.

4   Inhale deeply—the vibrant energy from this sphere is ready to permeate your body. As you exhale, imagine the energy washing down through your body, leaving through the soles of your feet into the ground. Repeat five times.

5   Visualize another ball of energy, below your feet in the Earth. This time the energy is a rich ruby red. Inhale as it radiates up into the base of your spine where it pulses, like a slow, steady heartbeat. Breathe into this sphere, slowly and steadily.

6   Now breathe the red energy in through your body, up to the very top of your head. Repeat this five times.

7   Stand still and notice how you feel. You may feel energy tingling or pulsing in your body.

LOOKING AT
THE CHAKRAS

You have just experienced the energy of the chakras—in particular the crown chakra (at the top of the head) and the base chakra (at the base of the spine). Now let's become acquainted with all seven of the major energy centers of the body.

THE BASE CHAKRA

The base chakra is located at the base of the spine and its color is red. It rules over the material world, our physical structure, and our social and financial position in life. When in balance, this chakra brings good health and energy, ease and relaxation. Imbalance may cause disorders of the bowel and intestines; problems with bones and teeth; eating disorders; problems with legs, feet, knees, base of spine, and buttocks.

DEFICIENT ENERGY
You may feel disconnected from your body and possibly be underweight. You lack focus and discipline and are disorganized. You're fearful, anxious, restless—you can't settle. You may have money worries.

EXCESSIVE ENERGY
You may overeat and be overweight. There's a tendency to hoard and to hold on. Energy levels may be low and you often feel sluggish and lazy. You are scared of change and crave security.

HEALING THE BASE CHAKRA
Try to reconnect with your body in any way you can. Find a form of exercise that you can enjoy—it doesn't matter what it is, as long as you enjoy it. Good bodywork and massage will help. Gardening and pottery are good grounding exercises. Look at your early relationship with your mother: talk to her about it, if you can—if self-reflection is painful, find a psychotherapist or counselor to talk to so that you can explore past issues safely.

THE SACRAL CHAKRA

The second chakra is located between the lower abdomen and the navel. Its color is orange and it deals with sensuality, sexuality, and relationships. When balanced, it enables you to be kind to yourself and others. You enjoy pleasure without guilt. If it's out of balance, you may suffer reproductive and urinary system issues; menstrual problems; lack of flexibility in the lower back and knees; sexual dysfunction; loss of appetite.

DEFICIENT ENERGY—
You may feel rigid and stiff. You could deny yourself pleasure and possibly have poor social skills. There may well be a lack of desire, passion and excitement in life, and you may lack interest in sex.

THE SOLAR PLEXUS CHAKRA

The third chakra is located above the navel. Its color is yellow and it deals with self-esteem, energy, will, confidence, and inner power. When balanced, you are warm, confident, self-assured without being arrogant, often playful, and spontaneous. If imbalanced, it can cause digestive and eating disorders, ulcers, muscular problems, chronic fatigue, hypertension, and diabetes. Weak points are the stomach, pancreas, gall bladder, and liver.

DEFICIENT ENERGY—
You will be low in physical and emotional energy and may have poor self-discipline and low self-esteem. You could be unreliable, overly passive, and easily manipulated. You could find yourself as a victim.

THE HEART CHAKRA

The fourth chakra is based in the heart and chest. Its color is green and it deals with issues of love, intimacy, balance, and relationships. When balanced, you are compassionate and loving, empathetic and altruistic, peaceful and balanced. Physical imbalance shows up in disorders of the heart, lungs, breasts, and arms. You may have asthma, circulation problems, or issues with your immune system.

DEFICIENT ENERGY—
Too little energy in this chakra can make you antisocial and withdrawn, critical and judgmental of others or yourself. It can cause depression, loneliness, and a fear of relationships.

EXCESSIVE ENERGY— You may be addicted to pleasure and sex. You may swing wildly between moods, having endless crises. Emotionally, you are oversensitive and overdependent on others.

HEALING THE SACRAL CHAKRA— Learn to trust and enjoy your senses. Be mindful of textures around you; listen to sounds; look at nature and art; taste different foods and drinks. Free dance can loosen up this chakra (try Gabrielle Roth's Five Rhythms or Biodanza). Get in touch with your emotions to release any old feelings of hurt, anger, and guilt (with professional help if necessary).

EXCESSIVE ENERGY— You may well be aggressive and domineering, manipulative, deceitful and controlling. You have driving ambition, are very competitive, arrogant, and exceedingly stubborn.

HEALING THE SOLAR PLEXUS CHAKRA— If you have a deficiency, start learning to take risks (with help if needed). Bodywork, self-compassion exercises and qigong could help. Strengthen your core with Pilates or yoga. If you have too much energy here, focus on mindfulness strategies (such as meditation, or autogenic training) and deep relaxation practices such as yoga nidra.

EXCESSIVE ENERGY— You may well be demanding, clingy, jealous, dependent, and overly self-sacrificing.

HEALING THE HEART CHAKRA— Breathing exercises will help all those with problems in the heart chakra. Check out workshops or classes which teach breathing (page 26). Start a journal—writing down all your feelings and thoughts honestly. Look at your relationships, and work at letting go of suppressed grief and loss (with professional help if necessary). Start to accept yourself—just as you are.

THE THROAT CHAKRA

The fifth chakra is located in the throat. Its color is blue and it deals with issues of communication and creativity. A well-balanced throat chakra shows in a resonant voice and clear communication. You have a great sense of timing and rhythm, are a good listener and have plenty of creativity in your life. Physically, imbalance shows disorders of the throat, ears, voice, neck, and tightness of the jaw.

DEFICIENT ENERGY—
You struggle to put your feelings into words; you are scared of speaking out and could be overly shy. Anyone who feels they are tone deaf or completely lacking rhythm should look at this chakra.

THE BROW CHAKRA

The sixth chakra is based in the forehead. Its color is indigo and it deals with imagination, intuition, dreams, and insights. A well-balanced brow chakra makes you intuitive and perceptive, with a good memory and imagination. Headaches, poor eyesight, or problems with vision arise when it is out of balance.

DEFICIENT ENERGY—
You may suffer from weak memory, vision, and lack of imagination. It's hard to remember dreams and you struggle to envisage the future. You may be rigid and dogmatic in your thoughts.

THE CROWN CHAKRA

The seventh chakra is found in the cerebral cortex of the brain. Its color is violet and it rules understanding and our connection with the divine. If well balanced, you'll be open-minded, thoughtful, and wise. You analyze and assimilate information easily. You have broad understanding and will generally have a sense of spiritual connection. Migraines and amnesia indicate issues in this Chakra.

DEFICIENT ENERGY—
You may be cynical, rigid, and tend to ridicule spirituality. You may be apathetic greedy and materialistic, trying to dominate others.

EXCESSIVE ENERGY—
You talk too much and can't listen. You gossip, interrupt, and are known for your loud, intrusive voice.

HEALING THE THROAT CHAKRA— Use your voice: singing, chanting, humming, shouting, sound therapy, or voicework are all helpful. If you have excessive energy, practice the art of silence and deep listening. Use bodywork to release tension in the neck and shoulders. The Alexander Technique, Feldenkrais, Pilates are all ideal. Write your thoughts and unspoken feelings in a journal; write letters (they don't have to be sent).

EXCESSIVE ENERGY—
You live too much in your dreams and imagination—you have difficulty concentrating and have frequent nightmares. You may be obsessive and even suffer delusions.

HEALING THE BROW CHAKRA— Try painting and drawing—use whatever materials and colors you like and paint whatever comes to mind (the results do not have to be artistic). Look at your painting and see what emotions emerge. Record and work with your dreams. Guided visualizations can be useful when healing the brow chakra—so can hypnotherapy (working with a qualified expert).

EXCESSIVE ENERGY—
You live too much in your head. You may have lost touch with your body and may be excessively spiritual or confused.

HEALING THE CROWN CHAKRA— Meditation is the key to healing the crown chakra. If you're deficient here, open your mind to new ideas and new information— don't dismiss things until you've tried them. Examine your attitude to spirituality. If you have an excess of crown chakra energy, connect with your body and the earth—through movement, massage, or gardening.

CONTACTING THE CHAKRAS THROUGH SOUND

Each chakra has its own sound and by toning it, we can get in touch with its individual energy. As you tone each sound feel it resonate through your body.

1   Stand or sit comfortably. Take a few deep groans to release your jaw and neck. Sigh and yawn to loosen up your mouth. Gently close your eyes and take your breath down to your abdomen as we did on page 23.

2   Visualize your base chakra, glowing red at the base of your spine. Breathe into it and make the sound "uh" (like a deep, resonant groan). Imagine the sound coming not just from your throat, but also from your base chakra. As one "uh" ends, breathe and start another. Keep going for as long as feels comfortable—around two minutes is ideal.

3   Now visualize your sacral chakra glowing orange below the navel. Make the sound "oooo"—deep but not as profound as the "uh". Feel it resonate in your genital area.

4   Visualize your solar plexus chakra, gleaming a bright pure yellow. Tone a mid-range "oh" (rhyming with so and go).

5   Your heart chakra glows with a soft shimmering green. The sound is slightly higher again—a soft and gentle "ah" (as in far). Feel your heart expand with love as the "ah" vibrates and expands.

<u>6</u> Your throat chakra glimmers a clear, pure blue. The sound is "eye" as in the word : "I". It is higher again, clear, and bell-like.

<u>7</u> Your brow chakra shines with a pure indigo. Tone the sound "ey" (as in "say"). Feel your third eye become energized by the sound, and your intuition be enlivened.

<u>8</u> Your crown chakra, at the top of your head, is pure purple. The sound here is the highest of all—a gentle, not shrill, "eee" (as in "me"). Feel that sound resonating in your crown chakra.

<u>9</u> Now imagine all the chakras linked together, with energy flowing smoothly between each of them—a glistening bolt of energy running right through the center of your body.

<u>10</u> Stand or sit quietly, when you have finished, and slowly allow yourself to come back to waking consciousness. Stamp your feet to ground yourself.

Practice this regularly. If you need help with the sounds, check out Jonathan Goldman's YouTube videos (www.youtube.com/watch?v=F8kwc1lkiAQ). Once you are familiar with this exercise, you can use it as a tuning fork for your chakras. Become aware of each chakra as you move your intention into it. Is the sound muddy or less clear for any particular chakras? What do you notice in each chakra?

HEALING THERAPIES FOR THE BODY

We know we have physical bodies—we can feel and touch them. Yet, we are far more than skin and bones. We are, fundamentally, energy beings—as recognized by ancient healing systems and proved by quantum physics. Energy medicine simply seeks to find the imbalances within your energy fields and bring them back into balance.

Vital energy is known in China as qi and in Japan as ki. In India it's known as prana and in the Middle East as quwa. The Chinese saw the body as a shimmering mass of energy flowing along lines known as meridians. In Ayurveda, a similar concept talks of the marmas.

While orthodox doctors may ignore the energy body, holistic practitioners take it very seriously, knowing that the balanced flow of energy is the linchpin to achieving or maintaining good health. Our bodies are always striving towards wellness—illness is simply the body's way of telling us that something is wrong at a more subtle level.

There are now hundreds of different ways to experience energy medicine—from acupuncture to zero balancing. They are all worth investigating and trying for yourself. Right now, let's look at just a few which you can easily and readily use.

SHIATSU—FINGER PRESSURE FOR SIMPLE HEALING

✳

In Japanese, shiatsu combines two words: *shi* (finger) and *atsu* (pressure). Simply, it is finger pressure. Shiatsu was one of the original forms of folk energy healing, used by everyone to treat members of the family. We practice an instinctive form of self-shiatsu every time we press our foreheads to relieve a headache, or pinch the bridge of our noses to ease eye strain.

There is a subtle art in applying pressure slowly and evenly. Practice this on yourself first before you work on others. Press down slowly, hold to a count of five and release slowly. You don't have to wiggle your thumb or make rapid circular movements, just press in and hold. Some people prefer a light pressure; others like quite a deep pressure.

FIRST STEPS IN SHIATSU

1   Find a tense or tight muscle on your leg. Place your hands on it and feel the warmth.

2   Place your thumb on the muscle and press down gradually. Don't jab. The slower you press, the deeper you can go. Hold the point and count to five. Release slowly. Repeat the exercise a couple of times. Now, move an inch or so along the muscle and try again. Move on another inch, and try again.

With practice you may feel increasing warmth, tingling, a release of tension, or pain. You are releasing blocked energy—it's that simple.

BANISHING HEADACHES

Blocked energy through the neck and shoulders can lead to headaches. Using these techniques, on a daily basis, works best as a preventative measure. Press the points to the count of five, release slowly, press again, and release. Repeat a few times.

1   Press the inside corners of each eye. Pinch the bridge of your nose to find the points.

2   Press under your eyebrows. Rest your head on your fingertips, if necessary.

3   Pinch along your eyebrows.

4   Fingers apart, grip your head (your palms roughly over your ears), and work over the top of your head and down your neck.

5   Draw soft circles on your temples (without pressure).

6   Anchor your thumbs under your occipital ridge, just behind your ears on your hairline. Tilt your head forward and back.

7   Squeeze the back of your neck.

8   Bunch your fists against your sacrum (lower back) and lean back or lie down on the floor and place a tennis ball under your sacrum.

9   Pinch your little toe and your big toe.

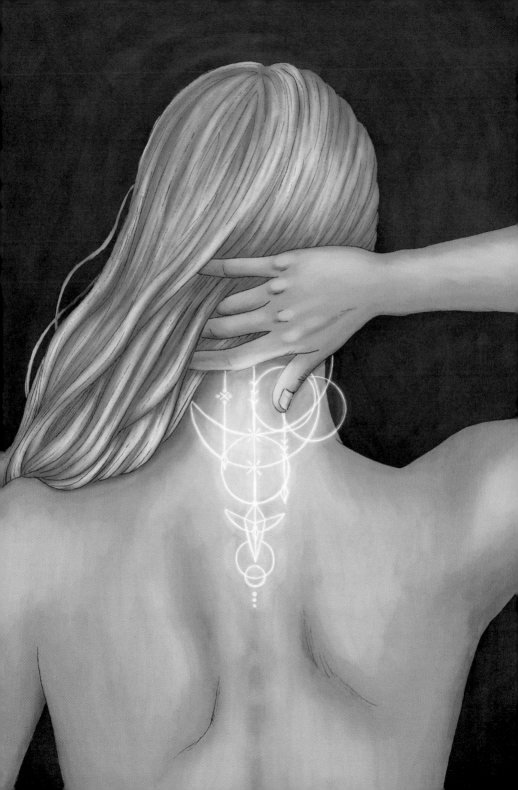

SOOTHING INSOMNIA

Curing chronic insomnia isn't a quick fix. Obviously, concentrate on sleep hygiene—switching off from devices and screens at least an hour before bed; making sure your bedroom is cool and dark; ensuring you don't eat or exercise too late in the day. You can also try this:

1   Lie on your back. Slide your fingers under your neck and apply gentle pressure.

2   Imagine your breath as a silver stream entering your left nostril, sitting at the top of your nose as you hold your breath to a count of five, and exiting your right nostril. Repeat.

3   Tighten your entire body, from the tips of your toes to your scalp. Release each part in turn.

BANISHING THE BLUES—BOOSTING ENERGY

"Pebble Therapy" is a great way to beat the blues and pick up your energy levels when you're feeling down. It is also good for poor circulation, or stiff joints.,

1   Take a handful of pebbles, roll them around in your palm, and squeeze them. Open and close your hand several times. Now squeeze the pebbles between your fingers.

2   Press your bare feet on them; roll the pebbles around the floor underfoot, and try picking them up between your toes.

HEALING

We can all heal—it's a skill that can be learned like any other. In fact, we might be healing every day, without even realizing. A mother rocking her baby sends healing energy to soothe and secure her child. A loving squeeze of the hand sends a boost of reassuring energy to a child heading off for school. A cool hand across a fevered forehead can help when someone is sick.

Some healers use specific holds and imagine certain symbols, as in Reiki, a Japanese form of healing. Some simply sit and think about their patient getting well, even though they are miles apart. Many healers insist they do not actively heal but merely open up the body so it can perform its own healing.

Once you can sense subtle energy, you simply need to be able to focus it through your hands.

AWAKENING YOUR HANDS

1   Rub your hands together quite vigorously for a few moments.

2   Now hold them a few inches apart—imagine you are holding a small ball. You may feel a tingling or warmth from your hands. Bounce your hands and feel the energy change as your hands move closer and further away.

3   Take your hands even further apart, as if you were holding, say, a football.

4   Now imagine that in the center of your palm is a circular area that can transmit energy. Rub it with the thumb of your other hand, visualizing it become activated. Repeat on the other hand. If you have any religious or spiritual beliefs you could call in for help on your healing quest.

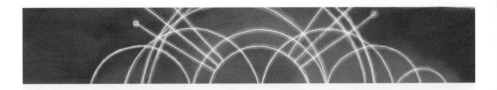

CHANNELING HEALING ENERGY

1   Stand in a relaxed position. Breathe slowly and deeply for a few minutes.

2   Visualize your chakras open and spinning in perfect harmony.

3   Now imagine you are pulling down vital energy through your crown chakra. The energy shoots through your body, linking up all the chakras. Spend a few moments allowing the energy to settle.

4   Breathe in the energy to your heart chakra. Think about your focus for this healing energy; ask to become a channel for this healing.

5   Visualize the energy shooting out from your heart along your arms to your hands. It tingles and buzzes, rippling along your fingers.

6   Now direct the energy to where it needs to be (either to a part of yourself or to someone else).

HEALING SOMEONE ELSE

1 Have the person you wish to heal standing, sitting, or lying down comfortably. Ask them to relax, close their eyes, and breathe naturally.

2 Run through the previous exercise. When you feel the energy coursing through your fingers, direct the healing energy to a part of your body. If a particular area is causing problems, hold your hands on or over that area. Visualize the healing energy streaming into that spot.

3 For a more general healing, simply let your hands move as they wish. You may feel drawn to touch a particular part of the body—or not to touch the body at all, keeping your hands a few inches away. Let your intuition guide you. You could focus on each of the chakras, visualizing your energy balancing each of them.

4 You might feel your hands become stiff or uncomfortable. Quietly shake them to release any negative energy you have picked up while working. Visualize the negative energy being absorbed by the Earth which can easily transform it.

ENERGY GAMES

The best way to learn about healing energy is to use it, practice it, and play with it. Try this exercise and enlist the help of a partner if you can.

1   Person one aims to direct energy to person two, while person two tries to resist it. It can be remarkably hard to resist receiving energy. If you are the person trying to give energy, how might you sneak past the other person's defences? If you are the person resisting, how could you protect yourself? These are useful techniques, as we will discover in later chapters. Sometimes it can be very useful to avoid energy!

2   Person one closes their eyes while person two directs energy to a particular part of their body. Person one guesses where the energy is being directed.

3   Person one lies down while person two scans their energy field. Guidance for person two: With your hands four or five inches above person one's body, run your hands from the top of the head down to the feet. Can you feel any areas of imbalance? What do you notice? Do any parts feel hot? Cold? Congested? What does your intuition tell you? Remember you are not diagnosing but sensing. Ask person one whether they have any discomfort or problems in the areas where you sensed something. Take it in turns to swap roles.

If someone has a pain, you can try to "draw it off": hold your hands over the spot and imagine the negative energy coming up into your hands. Gently shake it away and imagine it being absorbed and transformed into pure energy.

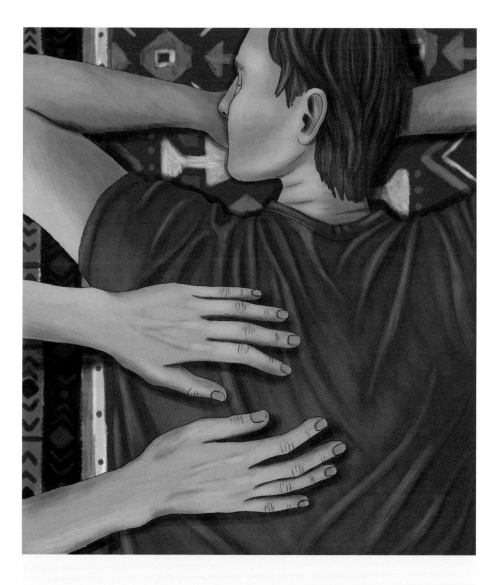

TAKING HEALING FURTHER

Once you have mastered the basics of healing, there are plenty of other techniques and props you can use to extend your healing repertoire. Experiment with some of the following to see which suit you best.

FLOWER ESENCES

Dr. Edward Bach, who developed the original Bach Flower Essences in Britain, believed that instead of ingesting the whole plant (as was traditional in herbalism or orthodox medicine), it would be more effective to take in the essence of the plant. Rather than dealing with the dense matter of flesh and blood, the remedies therefore go straight to the core of our being, our energetic body. As the Australian flower healer Ian White puts it, "The only difference between dense matter, such as antibiotics or a piece of wood, and subtle matter, such as a flower essence, is the frequency at which they vibrate. Subtle matter vibrates at speeds exceeding the speed of light."

I have been using flower essences for the past thirty years. They are totally safe to use—even on babies and animals—and really do bring about change. The remedies are readily available and you can slowly build up a collection. You simply choose the remedy or remedies (any number up to six or seven), which suit your current mood and add two drops of each to a 30ml "stock" bottle of fresh spring water. Traditionally, you would add a couple of drops of brandy as preservative. Then take four drops, four times daily, directly into your mouth or added to any drink.

THE BACH FLOWER REMEDIES

These are the main personality traits associated with the thirty eight remedies.

FEAR

ASPEN
Vague, undefined fears that something is wrong, or supernatural fears.

MIMULUS
Fear of known things—such as heights, spiders, meeting people.

CHERRY PLUM
Irrational thoughts and fears, fear of loss of control, or violent temper.

RED CHESTNUT
Overanxiety and fear for others.

ROCK ROSE
Sheer terror, sudden shocks, and alarms.

UNCERTAINTY

CERATO
Doubting one's own judgment.

GORSE
Hopelessness, pessimism.

GENTIAN
Despondent, discouraged.

HORNBEAM
Lack of energy, listless.

SCLERANTHUS
Indecisiveness, fluctuating moods.

WILD OAT
Lack of direction in life, uncertainty about career choices—very useful for teenagers and students.

LONELINESS

IMPATIENS
Impatience, irritability, or intolerance.

HEATHER
Self-obsession, hatred of being alone.

WATER VIOLET
Aloofness, disdain, or remoteness.

OVERSENSITIVITY

AGRIMONY
Torturing thoughts hidden behind cheerful façade.

CENTUARY
Timidity, subservience.

HOLLY
Envy, jealousy, hatred.

WALNUT
Difficulty adapting to change, good for rites of passage—puberty, menopause—or for shifts in circumstance, such as moving house or starting a new job.

DESPONDENCY OR DESPAIR

CRAB APPLE
Self-disgust, hatred of the body, or feelings of shame.

ELM
Strong and stoic but overwhelmed by responsibility.

LARCH
Lack of confidence, gives up easily.

OAK
Brave, determined, struggling against the odds.

PINE
Guilt, self-blame.

SWEET CHESTNUT
Extreme dispair.

STAR OF BETHLEHEM
For after-effects of severe shock.

WILLOW
Resentment, bitterness, or self-pitying.

OVERCONCERN FOR OTHERS

BEECH
Intolerant, critical, always has to be right.

CHICORY
Selfishness, possessiveness.

VERVAIN
Over-enthusiastic, fanatical.

VINE
Domineering.

ROCK WATER
Self-repression.

INSUFFICIENT INTEREST IN THE PRESENT

CHESTNUT BUD
Keeps repeating the same mistakes.

CLEMATIS
Excessive daydreaming.

HONEYSUCKLE
Nostalgia, lives in the past—often good for older people.

MUSTARD
Depression.

OLIVE
Exhaustion, burn-out.

WHITE CHESTNUT
Persistent worries.

WILD ROSE
Resignation, apathy.

SOUND
THERAPY

✦

We've already experienced the effects of sound therapy, in our chakra toning exercises. The ancient esoteric schools of India and Tibet, Greece, and Egypt, all taught the importance of the power of sound: vibration was held to be the basic creative force in the universe. The Bible says exactly that: "In the beginning was the Word" while the Kabbalah and the Vedas place precise and great importance on sounds and mantras.

Simply by making different sounds, you can affect your whole mood. Deep groaning is a great way to release negative emotions and can re-energize you if you're tired. If you're feeling tense, try softly humming to yourself. If you listen to young babies, one of the first sounds they make is a soft "mmmm"—it's a potent form of self-soothing.

"Disease is simply parts of our bodies vibrating out of tune," says pioneering sound therapist, Jonathan Goldman. "Every organ, bone, tissue and other parts of the body have a healthy resonant frequency. When that frequency alters, that part of the body vibrates out of harmony, and that is what is termed as disease. If it were possible to determine the correct resonant frequency for a healthy organ and then project it into that part which is ill, the organ should return to its normal frequency and a healing should occur."

Goldman firmly believes that by creating sounds, which are in harmony with the "correct" frequency of the healthy organ, we could entrain our bodies back into balance. So, practice the chakra toning exercise as often as you can (page 31).

COLOR THERAPY

✳

Color can affect everything in our lives. Red walls in a bar could mean more fights at closing time. Soft pink walls, on the other hand, have been found to make people less aggressive—it's used in some prisons and police "drunk tanks". Color directly affects the central nervous system, which controls our behavior. Since the 1940s, researchers have found that different colors produce different levels of arousal in the nervous system. Colors with long wavelengths, such as red, create higher levels of arousal than those with shorter wavelengths (such as green and blue).

Color therapists use lamps with different filters to flood the body with color, or to beam combinations of color onto specific points of the body. Some prescribe "color diets" or advise clients to dress in certain colors and decorate their houses in particular hues, to heal an array of physical and emotional conditions. It sounds far-fetched but a growing band of solid scientific research seems to back up the claims. Viewing certain colors actually evokes physical change. For example, going back to the red walls in the bar: seeing red can stimulate the glandular system and increase the heart rate, blood pressure, and respiration.

One of the best-known experiments in the use of color showed that patients with high blood pressure could lower their blood pressure on demand, simply by visualizing the color blue. Whereas when they visualized red, the blood pressure rose. Another study found that adult students with reading difficulties can be helped by using colored filters.

Dose yourself with spectrums of color as broad as possible. If your problems involve coldness, poor circulation, lethargy, or constipation you need to invoke the warmer colors—reds, oranges, yellows, and pinks. U.S. research even found that painting your bathroom in warm oranges and reds could help to cure constipation! On the other hand, if you are feverish or suffer from inflammation and "hot" conditions, then the soothing blue and green shades could quite literally cool you down.

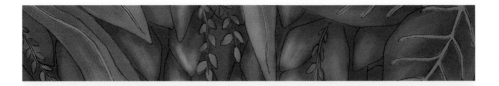

COLOR BREATHING

This exercise can be very healing. Do it for yourself when you are feeling under par, or direct someone else to use the exercise.

1   Lie down and make yourself comfortable.

2   Choose a color from the color correspondence list opposite.

3   Visualize the color you have chosen as a cloud, which you can slowly absorb through the pores of your skin. As you inhale, imagine the colored cloud entering your body through your fingers and toes, and then travelling throughout your body (visualize your bones as hollow so the color can seep through).

4   Then, as you exhale, imagine the color leaving your body, taking with it all sickness, toxins, and symptoms of illness. It all leaves your body and vaporizes harmlessly.

5   Repeat several times.

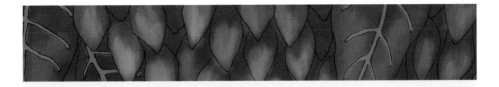

COLOR CORRESPONDENCE LIST

RED

Circulation, problems with the blood, sexual problems, ill-effects of cold, or numbness.

ORANGE

Depression, hernias, or kidney stones. Can help breastfeeding mothers by promoting better milk flow.

YELLOW

Indigestion, constipation, or diabetes. Supports the lymphatic system, kidneys, and liver.

GREEN

Nervous conditions, colds, flu, ulcers, or hay fever.

TURQUOISE

Throat problems—anti-inflammatory.

BLUE

Excellent for pain relief, for bleeding and burns, colics, respiratory problems, skin problems, and rheumatism.

INDIGO

Migraine, ear and eye problems, skin disorders, and nervous system failure.

VIOLET

Emotional problems, arthritis, can ease childbirth.

MAGENTA

Heart and mental problems.

THE ENERGETIC
POWER OF FOOD

CHAPTER FOUR

If you want to cultivate vital energy in your life, pay attention to what you eat. The energy of food doesn't come just from the actual foods we choose to eat (although that is important)—it also comes from how we cook our food, how we eat our food, or even how we think about food.

Our understanding of how food affects us is growing all the time. It is now well known that our gut is our "second brain" and that ninety per cent of the body's natural "feel good" neurotransmitter, serotonin, is made in the digestive tract. We are also learning that conditions previously regarded as purely psychological, such as depression, can be triggered by inflammation in the body and, in particular, the gut.

Ancient cultures had specific guidelines for eating, informed by complex philosophies that ensured maximum energy for the body. Ayurveda, for example, teaches that a subtle energy substance, called "ojas", is extracted from food once it has been perfectly digested (emphasize "perfectly"). Ojas imbue our cells with energy. In effect, it makes them feel happy. The ideal diet is what Ayurveda calls "sattvic" food—foods that promote life, health, happiness, and satisfaction; it helps us become serene and contented; it balances our energies.

In a nutshell, sattvic foods are prepared, sourced as locally and seasonally as possible. Ideally, it would be organic and vegetarian, light and easily digested.

Ayurveda also teaches that the way you eat is of importance too. Although food should always taste good, it also needs to attract the other senses, so think about foods that smell great and feel good in the mouth. Make sure your plate looks attractive—and your table as well.

Like Ayurveda, Traditional Chinese Medicine (TCM) teaches the importance of good eating for optimum energy. Food is so important that many traditional physicians will cure illness using food as the primary tool—an idea that's resurfacing with the rise of functional (lifestyle) medicine. Only if the disease is very resistant will the physician move on to using herbs or, as a last resort, acupuncture. Good food is considered good medicine and, as with all Chinese therapy, the aim is to achieve an optimum balance of energy.

In TCM, as in Ayurveda, food is considered to release a vital essence—it is seen specifically as an alchemical act, whereby essential nutrients are transformed into energy. The key to energy exchange in food is believed to lie with enzymes. "Enzymes are endowed with a spark of living energy, or qi, and this energy gives them their remarkable bioactive powers," said Daniel Reid, author of several Chinese healing books. He warns that modern farming and food-processing methods often produce foods that are lacking in minerals, vitamins, and enzymes—or that essential spark. No wonder so many of us lack vitality and crave sugar and simple carbs, desperate for an energy fix.

SPIRIT AND
SOUL FOOD

———————— ✦ ————————

If you are interested in finding out more about the sattvic diet or the TCM way of eating, you will find plenty of information online or in specialist cookbooks. What isn't so readily available is information about something much more esoteric—how the way we cook and eat our food affects its vital energy. Does it really matter whether we lovingly chop our vegetables by hand, or simply chuck them in the food processor? Does it make a difference if we sit down, say a blessing, and mindfully eat our food rather than chomp it absentmindedly while watching Netflix? Apparently it does.

Almost every spiritual tradition, whether Sufi, Native American, Jewish, Christian, Hindu, or Muslim, regards food as sacred—and the eating of food as a sacrament. The Sufis, for example, hold that our health and happiness are affected by what goes on in our kitchens. Yet in our frantic modern-day society, food has been reduced to "fuel". Many of our food-related issues, from overeating to anorexia, can be traced back to a lack of awareness of the relationship between body and soul. We have lost our spiritual connection to the food we eat: we have lost the energetic link.

Research has found that how food is prepared can actually affect its nutritional content and taste. The way we eat our food and the attitude we bring to it, can make a difference to how it is metabolized.

Physicist Fred Alan Wolf Ph.D. says it is insufficient to ask, "What nutrients are in the food?" Rather, we should be asking, "What were you thinking about when you were eating?" A new scientific field is in the making— one that may give us a prescription for creating an as yet unidentified "nutrient" that manifests through the wisdom and awareness we bring to our food. Maybe this is the ojas of Ayurveda? By combining intention, visualization and healing energy, food can be transformed—it can actually be found to contain more vitality, and more healing powers. Leonard Laskow M.D., author of *Healing with Love*, found that projecting loving energy to an orange actually changed the taste and texture of the fruit—it peeled more easily and was sweeter and juicier. Cheap wine

took on the taste of a classic vintage. Research biochemist Bernard Grad Ph.D., discovered that a person's state of mind could affect the growing capacity of seeds; while Larry Dossey M.D., author of *Healing Words*, found that focused prayer could keep milk fresh longer.

Try the following to test whether you can detect the energetic difference between ordinary food and foods imbued with spiritual energy.

Processed versus hand prepared vegetables. Make a salad—chop half of the vegetables mindfully, using a knife and cutting board; chop the other half in a food processor. Can you detect the difference in the experience of eating the different types of salad?

Cooking consciously versus unconsciously. Before enjoying a favorite dish, shop for, prepare, cook, and eat the food with a loving consciousness. As a contrast, next time you prepare the same dish, choose to do so during an especially busy time—do everything in a hurry, without any care or thought. Can you notice any difference in the experience of enjoying the meal?

CREATING FOODS WITH LOVING ENERGY

1 Sit or stand in a comfortable position. Become aware of your breathing.

2 Focus your attention on your heart chakra. Think of people you love, of wonderful moments in your life—anything that bring up loving, caring feelings.

3 Now visualize a shimmering sphere of light, several inches above your head. This is the crown chakra. The powerful energy from this sphere comes down into your head and descends through the chakras into your heart and hands.

4 Now project this wonderful healing energy into the food or drink before you. The light comes out through your heart and hands and soaks into the food. Surround both sides of the dish with your hands and feel the energy emanating from both of your hands, pouring into the food or drink.

5 Pause for a moment, giving thanks for the gift of this transformative energy.

SOUL SHOPPING
AND SPIRITUAL COOKERY

As the most energetically pure food is fresh, seasonal, and organic, why not think about growing (at least some of) your own food? Even if you don't have a garden or allotment, you can grow a window box of herbs, pop a few grow bags for tomatoes or peas on your porch or balcony. Lettuce grows happily in hanging baskets, beans will clamber up a wall with the help of some trellis. If you can't grow your own, try buying your food from local suppliers, farmers' markets, or via organic box schemes.

Wherever you live, become conscious of how and when you shop, and how much you buy. We're all busy, but making time to buy food as and when you need it, rather than doing a huge shop each week and stuffing most of it in the freezer, will encourage you to eat more fresh food and reduce waste. Take time in deciding what you would like to cook and eat. Be conscious when choosing your produce—pick each vegetable with awareness. Notice its shape, texture, and scent. Think about where the food has come from and imagine it in its original surroundings.

Most of us rarely stop to consider the origins of our food. We abnegate responsibility—we accept food that has been genetically modified and irradiated, stuffed with preservatives, pesticides, and hormones. When you start to think more deeply about where your food comes from, you may find your eating habits totally change. Who created the mass-produced soup in the can? Did they lovingly slice the vegetables, chop the herbs with care, stir the soup with love and awareness? Unlikely, isn't it? So, make your own "soul soup", preparing each ingredient with mindfulness and permeate the dish with love as you prepare it. You might say a prayer for each person who will eat it, imagining that you are cooking a magical pot with healing powers. You could bake "conception cookies" for someone who is trying to conceive but having difficulty. "Love porridge" to catch the heart of the person you want to attract. Fanciful right? Remember that researching how our thoughts and prayers can affect food. Just try it.

MAKE
MEALTIMES SPECIAL

✳

In days gone by, mealtimes were times of gathering, when families and extended family and friends came together. It was a time of discussion, sharing stories, giving advice and sympathy, of laughter, and sometimes tears. Now, we rarely eat together and we miss out on the communal energy of the shared table. Very simple things can make mealtimes special. Think about the appearance of your meals and lay your table with care, attention, and imagination.

Ponder on how you can make each person feel comfortable. Seating plans may seem old-fashioned but there is magic in deciding on who sits where. The place at the top of the table is traditionally the place of honor—if you want to show respect, place your grandparents, or parents there. Difficult children can be kept in line by being placed next to them.

Dining outdoors brings an elemental (sometimes unpredictable) energy to mealtimes. Enjoy a picnic—in the woods, on the beach, up a mountain, in a city park, or on a boat floating on a lake. It doesn't have to be hot and it doesn't need to be daytime. Transform a garden or roof terrace into a magical outdoor room with loads of candles in jars or storm lanterns. Wrap up warm and have a winter barbecue. Don't forget to sing songs and tell tales after the meal—in the best campfire tradition.

Bring back the old art of blessings and grace to mealtimes. It does not need to be religious or long-winded. Sharing a moment of thanks is a way of making us conscious of the food we eat and the way it came to our table. Use it as a form of mindfulness.

Make your mealtimes warm, loving, and peaceful occasions. One ritual (either quietly on your own or enlisting the help of everyone) is to visualize the table surrounded by a loving ball of vital energy. I see it as a soft golden pink, but you could choose whichever color you prefer. Imagine there is a cord coming from the heart chakra of each person, into the center of the table where they meet and entwine. Everyone is linked in a swirling network of light and energy. This is a particularly useful meditation if you have a difficult family mealtime ahead of you.

ENERGY
EXERCISE

CHAPTER FIVE

We all know that exercise is good for both body and mind—it tones our hearts and lungs, promotes healthy bones, and releases the feel-good chemicals that boost our mood. Yet, energy exercise is not about gearing up for triathlons or enduring boot camps. It's about finding mindful ways of getting vital energy to course through your body. In fact, plenty of exercises in this chapter involve a little more than standing in one spot. Not too arduous?

Many of us were put off sport when we were at school because we just weren't very good at what was offered. How many of us were humiliated on the running track, or dredged up or made excuses not to be put through the shame of failing yet again at gym? I loathed sports at school because I simply wasn't the gymnastic type.

The key is to find something you love; something that you find fun, rather than a drudge. Often you may be surprised at what you love.

Years ago, I went on a bodywork retreat weekend where we tested out a whole range of exercise forms. I was stunned to find that I loved Zumba and enjoyed the challenge of kettlebells; that I could do interval training and that Fitness Pilates was tough but exhilarating.

EXERCISE AS MEDITATION

Think about using exercise as a form of meditation. The easiest way to do this is to start with walking.

1 As you walk, become aware of placing your feet on the ground. At first, you can say to yourself, "right foot, left foot," as you feel each foot touch the ground.

2 How does the ground feel? Make yourself as light as possible, so you literally tread lightly upon the Earth. Try to keep breathing through your nose—this may mean you slow down your pace a little to begin with.

ANCIENT EXERCISES
TAILOR-MADE FOR TODAY

✳

Yoga, qigong, and tai chi are all forms of pure energy exercises. More than that, they are also profound healing methods. Just as Chinese physicians preferred to use food ahead of more aggressive healing methods, so they would also prescribe qigong which, with its combination of breathing, posture, and meditation, could influence every part of the body, from the inside out. The very name "qigong" translates as "working with life energy". It is a profound science, which can pinpoint energy imbalances and correct them.

Absolutely anyone can do qigong. If you are unable to stand up, you can perform the exercises sitting down. Ideally, you should practice qigong every day, even for only five or ten minutes. It is not a quick fix, but the more often you practice it, the more energy it will generate. While other forms of exercise often take away your energy, qigong increases it. You will find your body shape changing as a result of the combined effects of qigong breathing, movement, and the liberation of qi.

If you find these following exercises enjoyable, it would be worth finding a teacher and pursuing it further.

THE STARTING POSTURE

This posture helps you become aware of your entire body. If it seems familiar it's because we started the book with a modified version of this position.

1 Stand with your feet shoulder-width apart. Find your natural balance—your weight should be neither too far forward nor too far back.

2 Feel the rim of your foot, your heel, your little toe, and big toe gently touching the ground.

3 Keep your knees relaxed and check that they are exactly over your feet.

4   Relax your lower back. Soften your stomach and buttocks.

5   Let your chest become hollow. Relax and slightly round your shoulders.

6   Imagine you have a high pigtail on the crown of your head which is tied to a rafter on the roof. Let your head float lightly and freely. Soften your tongue, mouth, and jaw.

7   Stay in this position for a few minutes with your hands hanging loosely by your sides.

8   Take your mind through the five elements. Earth (imagine the feeling of weight and rootedness); Water (think of looseness and fluidity); Air (a feeling of lightness and transparency); Fire (sparkle—remember this should be fun!); and Space (envisage the space within each joint, muscle, breath, and your mind).

9   Throughout your practice, keep bringing your mind gently back to your posture, this keeps the mind restful.

TURNING THE HEAD AND TWISTING THE TAIL

This exercise helps to improve kidney energy. It strengthens the spine, keeping it flexible and strong. It takes a fair bit of coordination but do persist, as it is highly effective.

1   Stand in the starting position (*see* page 70) with your arms raised at the side of the body to shoulder height.

2   Push your weight into the right leg, keeping both legs bent. Lean to the left while raising your right arm slightly. Allow the left arm to curve downwards so the tip of your fingers touch your left thigh about where a trouser seam would be. Turn your head to look into the palm of the right hand. As you perform this move, exhale.

3   Come back to the starting position, with your arms raised to the side of your body, breathing in as you return.

4   Now shift your weight into the left leg and lean to the right, raising your left arm slightly and curving the right arm downwards so the fingertips touch the right thigh. Turn your head to look into the palm of the left hand. Breathe out as you perform this move.

5   Repeat at least five times each side, keeping your movement slow and flowing.

DRAGON STAMPING

This exercise works wonders for your circulation, balance, and for both mental and physical energy. It helps to calm the mind and, if performed every morning, helps you become focused and energized for the day ahead. Make sure you are breathing out as you rise and breathing in as you return—it's very easy to get this the wrong way round which is far less effective.

1   Stand in the starting position (*see* page 70).

2   Breathing out, go slowly right up onto your tiptoes, as high as you can. Stretch your body upwards through your back, keeping the abdomen relaxed. At the same time, point your fingers down and inwards, stretching your arms downwards.

3   Return your heels slowly to the ground while inhaling and relax. Repeat at least five times.

YOGA—
MOBILIZING ENERGY

From a quick glance at Instagram you would think that everyone is doing yoga—and that everyone practicing it is a slim, super-bendy supermodel. Let's lose that image. Please. Let's get back into the "real" yoga—an energetic system that originally helped prepare students for meditation.

A good regular yoga practice will make you more flexible and also, more importantly, will put you in touch with your body, bringing you into the present moment. It can also put you in touch with your emotions, if you work consciously. Some people would say that yoga is equivalent to therapy.

"Yoga is a systematic approach to living with awareness and sensitivity," says international yoga teacher Tashidowa. "It's not uncommon for someone to feel tears flow during class as the process of stretching, twisting, and moving the body reveals and opens our emotional, psychological, and energetic blocks."

One of the surprising ways it does this is by tapping directly into our memories, at a cellular level. "Our muscle cells retain memories, which can be released through movement or by bringing the body into particular positions, such as the asanas," says Helga Himmelsbach, a yoga teacher in Ireland.

There are so many types of yoga, you may need to try a few different approaches before you find the one that suits you. It's a very individual choice. I'd suggest checking out different forms on YouTube first to narrow down your selection. Then drop in on a few different classes to road test them. Your choice of teacher is just as important as the form of yoga—so don't worry if you need to shop around a bit.

Always tell your teacher if you have any health issues, injuries, or if you are pregnant. Above all, never push yourself too far—the aim is to find your "edge", where you can feel the stretch without any pain. It is perfectly possible to injure yourself with yoga—all of my own exercise injuries have come from pushing myself too far in yoga!

WHICH YOGA WOULD SUIT ME?

YOU'RE AN ABSOLUTE BEGINNER

HATHA YOGA - Expect relaxation, warm-up, postures, breathing, and deep relaxation. Many teachers will also include meditation. This exercise is ideal for everyone and is the most commonly available class.

VINIYOGA - Tends to be taught one to one. It's a gentle and highly individualized form of yoga that is tailored to your personal needs, both physical and emotional. Students learn to adapt poses and set goals to build their own practice. It fosters self-awareness but in a very structured, safe environment. The perfect introduction for anyone nervous about yoga.

YOU WANT SOMETHING CLEAR AND PRECISE

IYENGAR YOGA—A very focused and precise form of yoga, which puts great emphasis on correct posture. Teachers use "props" such as blocks and belts to help you into position. Great for those who want the benefits without too much "weird stuff".

YOGA THERAPY—A therapeutic form of yoga with a medical background. The teacher will usually offer classes geared towards specific problems and conditions (such as back pain, arthritis, asthma, or pregnancy) and individual sessions if necessary. Yoga therapy is the best choice if you have a medical condition.

YOU WANT SOMETHING HOLISTIC

SIVANANDA YOGA—A gentle, laid-back form of yoga based around twelve key postures. It includes a strong, spiritual element (often with chanting and meditation). Sivananda yoga is ideal if you're deeply drawn to Indian philosophy and lifestyle.

DRU YOGA—A very gentle, holistic approach which includes breathing, visualization, deep relaxation, and meditation. Dru yoga uses graceful flowing movement sequences and is said to release negative thought patterns, energy blocks, and deep-seated trauma. Think of it as "yoga meets psychotherapy".

YOU GET EASILY BORED

ASHTANGA YOGA (VINYASA, POWER YOGA)—Ashtanga uses a specific breathing technique and sequences of postures carried out at far greater speed than other forms of yoga. It provides an intense workout. Although ashtanga seems the very antithesis of a soothing yoga practice, sometimes if we're overly stressed, it becomes impossible to relax into more meditative practice. Ashtanga is ideal for those who find "normal" yoga too slow and boring.

BIKRAM YOGA (HOT YOGA)—For this intense and athletic yoga style, the yoga studio is heated to a temperature of 35–42°C (95–108°F) to allow students to stretch that bit further. Practice with caution.

YOU WANT SOMETHING STRONG BUT SPIRITUAL

ANUSARA YOGA—This form has taken much from Iyengar yoga but adds a far more spiritual element. It's been called "Iyengar with a sense of humor". Rather than trying to get everyone to perform exactly the same postures, your teacher will guide you to express yourself to your best ability and in the way that feels most right for you. With the right teacher, this is a strong class that focuses on opening your heart.

JIVAMUKTI YOGA—The physical element of Jivamukti yoga is extremely physical and challenging, focusing on vinyasas (flowing sequences of postures). Yet, there is also a very strong spiritual element and each class has a theme. Expect to go way beyond postures into chanting and music (nada yoga), meditation, readings, and devotional affirmations.

YOU ARE TOTALLY EXHAUSTED

YIN YOGA—A yin yoga class is slow and meditative; you will hold postures for some considerable periods of time—often around five minutes or more. Because the postures are held for such a long time, they massage deep into the body, affecting not just the muscles and joints, but also the organs of the body. This approach also brings emotions up for acknowledgement.

YOGA NIDRA—Often practiced at the end of a standard class, yoga nidra is now available as a stand-alone practice. It is the yoga of sleep and profound relaxation. You lie in savasana (corpse pose) and are gently guided through the equivalent of a total sleep cycle. The practice is deeply restorative.

THE ENERGY
OF THE DANCE

As long as we humans have been able to walk, we have danced. From the active meditation of the whirling dervishes to the heartbeat rhythms of African dance, cultures across the world have moved to music. From the sultry sexuality of the tango to the serenity of circle dancing, we have used dance as a way to express our emotions and link the human body with mind and soul.

In many ancient cultures, dance was considered to be a way to communicate with the gods; a means of getting in touch with universal energy; a form of healing. "Dancing is a primal way to reach altered states of consciousness," says shaman Leo Rutherford. "To reach out of the confines of everyday life. Dancing helps us to return fully into our body and take our body to spirit."

The Kung San of the Kalahari Desert use ceremonial dance to activate "num", their term for vital energy. Num, they believe, is stored in the lower abdomen and at the base of the spine (akin to the Chinese dan tien and the Indian concept of kundalini). The Bushmen go into trance states following medicine dances all night, the aim of which is to make the num "boil"—at this point it can be projected into other people for healing.

Nowadays, you don't need to travel far to access forms of healing dances. There has been an explosion of free-form dance classes, where you don't have to learn steps and there is no right or wrong. The late Gabrielle Roth's Five Rhythms (originally called Life Dancing), aims to release emotions, reprogramme neural pathways, and access hidden sources of creativity, energy, and joy. Shakti dance came from kundalini yoga and is more structured yet still free and flowing. Qoya merges dance, yoga, and therapy with varying segments—it's a beautiful way to be seen as you truly are. Then there's Biodanza.

BIODANZA

Biodanza was created by Chilean psychologist and anthropologist Rolando Toro in 1960. He recognized that tribal societies have always used dance as a way to express deep feelings; to connect both with one another and to society as a whole. Dance is an energy exchange. Toro felt that by dancing in a manner true to our essential inner self, we could literally dance ourselves back to wholeness, by coming to accept our bodies and learning to feel more comfortable with our fellow human beings.

He found that certain kinds of music evoked certain kinds of movements which, in turn, brought about quite pronounced physiological and emotional changes. Some stimulated the sympathetic nervous system; others the parasympathetic nervous system. All affected our energy. Toro came to believe that each of us have five different energetic modes of living:

VITALITY—Feeling energy, facing the world.

AFFECTIVITY—Feelings of love, tenderness, and respect; giving and receiving love energy from other people.

SEXUALITY—Deriving pleasure from our sensual energy.

CREATIVITY—Bringing creative energy into everyday life.

TRANSCENDENCE—Going beyond ego to find something powerful outside ourselves.

Our problems arise, Toro hypothesized, because we stifle or block out some or all of these experiences so we fall out of natural balance. The aim of Biodanza is to bring the whole person back into a childlike sense of wholeness, by stimulating underdeveloped areas of feeling and bringing all five into balance. There is absolutely no need to be a "good" dancer when practicing Biodanza, the whole point is to find your own dance.

HOME DANCE CLASS

Try the following exercises to experience a taste of Biodanza in your own home.

1 Walk around the room and start to connect with your body. Feel your feet connecting firmly with the ground; let your arms swing naturally and keep your head up high. Gradually let your movement become more fluid, more vital, more exuberant.

2 Put on music with a strong but fluid melody. Dance in any way you choose, focusing on your heart and allowing your dance to be led from that area.

3 Next, change the music to something with a solid, firm bass rhythm. This time let your movements be governed by your pelvic region.

4 Play with finding your "own" dance. Forget notions of what you think dancing should look like. Allow the music to dance you—you might end up jumping in the air, or rolling on the floor—it doesn't matter.

5 Now give your dance to someone else. If you are trying these exercises with a friend, one of you should sit on the floor and "receive" the dance while you dance for him/her. If you are doing this alone, imagine you are dancing for someone special and pretend they are sitting in front of you. Concentrate on really giving the other person what they might need. Maintain eye contact all the way through the exercise. Then swap over and receive their dance.

✳

EMOTIONAL
ENERGY

———————

WORKING WITH
EMOTIONAL ENERGY

CHAPTER SIX

You wake up and it's Monday morning. You are dreading a meeting with a person you hate. How do you feel? Now, imagine you wake up and it's Saturday morning: ahead of you lies a day at the beach with your family or a group of great friends. Does that feel different? You bet it does! Learning how to shift your emotional energy can be a huge boon in modern life. It won't take the traumas and unpleasantness out of everyday life but it will enable you to deal with it in the best way possible.

Emotional energy manifests in our moods, our feelings, and attitudes. If vital energy moves through you freely, you will tend to have a sunny disposition, an optimistic outlook, a frank, open and honest approach to the world. If your energy is blocked, you will probably experience what we tend to call "toxic" emotions: for example, anger, fear, jealousy, resentment, or shame.

Many therapists now think that our emotional energy can become blocked, warped, or repressed at a very early age. In fact, research shows that we pick up patterning in the womb and can even hold generational trauma, inherited from several generations back. It's now known that traumatic events in someone's life can change the way their DNA is expressed and that change can be passed on to the following generations. This growing field is called "epigenetics". To be clear, the DNA code itself does not change but rather chemical tags are added or deleted from our DNA in response to our experiences. Researchers now believe that wars, famines, and genocides can leave an epigenetic mark on the descendants of those who actively experienced them. For example, a 2015 study showed that children of Holocaust survivors had epigenetic changes to a gene linked to cortisol, a key stress hormone.

Take a few moments to consider the following questions:

What emotions surrounded your conception and the news of your existence? Ask your parents if you can. If not, is there anyone else you can ask? Siblings, aunts, uncles, your parents' friends?

———

What is your emotional heritage? Did your ancestors go through trauma or have any emotional or mental health issues?

———

How was your mother's pregnancy—physically, emotionally? Was there any stress? Were there any financial worries?

What kind of birth did you have? How was your early childhood? What is your earliest memory?

———

What do you remember most about your childhood? What emotions did you express most freely? Which emotions were you not allowed, or not encouraged to express?

———

Did you suffer any traumas as a child? Did you lose a parent or witness your parents' divorce? Was there illness in the family, or poverty, or severe stress?

It is worth making the effort to dig out this information. As babies and children, we are incredibly open to suggestion: we are like little psychic sponges. Equally, we can find ourselves carrying the trauma of previous generations—the depression, shame, fear ,and anger of our forebears. However, the good news is that this legacy is not a life sentence. The system is malleable and researchers believe that we also have the capacity to heal the effects of trauma, preventing it from echoing down through future generations. Developmental biologist Bruce Lipton, author of The Biology of Belief, firmly believes that we can manipulate our DNA by our thoughts and beliefs. "We are the creators of our situation," he said in an interview with SFGate (www.sfgate.com). "Genes are merely the blueprints. We are the contractors, and we can adjust those blueprints. We can even rewrite them."

TRACKING UNWANTED
EMOTIONAL ENERGY

───────────────── ✳ ─────────────────

This exercise helps uncover underlying negative emotions that stifle energy flow. Choose a time when you won't be disturbed, ideally somewhere where you can make a noise if you want to. You might choose to have some cushions or pillows around you. If you feel overly anxious about doing this exercise, have someone with you who you trust totally. If it feels very scary, you may need to explore this area with some professional help.

1   Lie down on the floor, on a comfortable mat or rug.

2   Spend some time breathing slowly and deeply.

3   Become aware of your body. Where are you holding tension? Where do you feel discomfort? Pinpoint the place and the feeling.

4   Now exaggerate the feeling. So, if you are clenching your jaw, clench it harder.

5   What does your body want to do or say? Don't think; just let your body follow its need. You might find yourself spitting out words or phrases; you might curl up in a ball; you might lash out at a cushion; you might do nothing.

6   Give your body permission to do whatever it needs in order to express its repressed emotional energy— within safe limits.

7   When you feel your body has had enough for this session, lie quietly once more and return to your breathing.

8   Stand up and stamp your feet to return to normal awareness. You may wish to write down what happened.

The issues you are dealing with may not be clear during the first time you try this. It may be worth rereading the section on chakras, since the areas of the body where we hold tension are often directly related to our emotional blockages.

As a brief guide:

THE EYE AREA tends to be about what we are allowed to see.

THE MOUTH, JAW, AND THROAT AREA tends to be about communication, about being heard, and about nourishment.

THE CHEST AND HEART AREA tends to be about anger, sadness, rejection, or longing.

THE ABDOMINAL AREA tends to be about fear and digestion (what we take in).

THE PELVIC/SACRAL AREA tends to be about sexuality, survival, support, or vitality.

Our bodies really do know the answers. Bodyworkers have found that repressed thoughts, feelings, old hurts, and memories are all stored in the body. If you feel you have a lot of old psychological "baggage" but are nervous of trying psychotherapy, I would heartily recommend you go to a good bodyworker. Many people find that under the skilled hands of a therapist, they can release old patterns, allowing emotional energy to run free. Sometimes you recall old hurts—at other times you don't need to relive the experience, you just let it go.

KEEP A JOURNAL – RECORD YOUR DREAMS

Do keep a journal of your experiences and feelings. It doesn't need to be beautiful or even well written; simply use it to record what you discover as a result of using the exercises in this book. Use it to jot down your stray thoughts, meditations, and your dreams.

Why record dreams? Dreams offer incredible pointers to help to understand our subconscious, but it can take some time to figure out their language. Dreams are expressed in riddles, symbols, and images rather than in straightforward messages. So, write down your dream and then spend some time thinking about it, however silly it might appear.

1 Animals and objects: If some particular object or animal appears in your dream, think about what it means to you. What significance does it have? What does it remind you of? Allow your mind to work laterally.

2 Other people: When other people appear in dreams, they often represent aspects of ourselves—perhaps those which are repressed or not allowed to express themselves freely. Animals can represent our "wild" side too. A great technique for understanding this form of energy is to hold a "conversation" with a character or an animal in a dream. Imagine it is sitting opposite you (behind a solid glass wall, if it's scary). Ask what it wants, what it needs.

3   Dream on: Another technique is to "dream the dream on". Lie or sit down and breathe slowly and calmly. Imagine yourself back in your dream. Run through the dream as you remember it but, instead of it ending, allow it to continue. What might happen next?

4   Paint your dreams: You don't need to be an artist to paint your dreams—far from it. Simply use a large piece of paper and whatever materials you fancy. Either draw your dream figuratively or just let the paint express how you felt in the dream. Don't censor yourself—if you feel that happening try painting with your nondominant hand, or with a blindfold. Notice any emotions that arise. After you have finished, sit back and look. What can you see? Maybe write to your painting—or dance the feelings it brings up in you.

These are all very powerful techniques and we're rushing through them at a rate of knots. Don't feel you have to do everything at once. Try each technique at your own pace. Time is one of the dimensions with which our energy was moulded from a very tender age. Many of us, in childhood, were constantly told to either "hurry up" or "slow down". So now, give yourself the time you need. Remember also that these techniques are often used in a therapeutic setting, with trained therapists to hand.

I tend to follow the belief of the great spiritual workshop leader Denise Linn, who believes that we will go no further than we are ready to—and that our psyches have a way of protecting us from going too far, too quickly. If you feel happy about these exercises, then you should be perfectly okay to do them. If you feel the slightest doubt, proceed with caution, or not at all.

LIBERATING
EMOTIONAL ENERGY

By now, you should have some idea of where your emotional energy blockages are and how they got there. Now, the work begins to shift them. First and foremost, remember that the blocks are there for good reason. Your energy is trying to protect you. So, thank the energy for being so protective and clever in thinking up ways of holding back painful memories and old hurts. Then, ask your inner self whether you are willing to let go. Tell your emotional energy blocks that you are ready to move on, to become more open, more vulnerable, and yes—less protected. You may find you feel a sense of something lifting, shifting, and moving away from you. Bless it and imagine it dispersed in a flash of white shimmering light, transmuted into something pure and able to return to the source.

Energy which has been lodged for years may not be so easy to shift. Like a stubborn stain, it might take weeks, months, or even years to resolve. Don't hurry over this. Let progress evolve naturally. You have a host of tools to help dissolve old stuck energy (a choice of energy "cleansers").

YOUR ENERGY CLEANSERS

BREATHE—Try practicing breathing exercises on a regular basis. If you have an area of the body or an emotion that feels stuck, try breathing into it, visualizing healing energy to clear away the blocks.

DANCE—Allowing your body to move as it wants can be hugely effective. Start with the Biodanza moves on page 80, and just let your body move in the way it wants to. You could also persist with the energy awareness exercise earlier in this chapter, exaggerating the movements (see page 86).

PAINT—Continue painting in a completely free fashion. Try the tips for loosening up your painting (see page 89).

DREAM – Continue with a dream diary and work with the images and symbols you discover (see page 88).

REFLECT: Find a good bodyworker or psychotherapist. Ideally, someone trained in both therapeutic talking and touching. Many bodyworkers are now training in counseling too.

DEALING WITH
OTHER PEOPLE'S ENERGY

✳

When we are functioning in line with our true nature, we gain a wonderful clarity, rather than remaining behind the walls, screens, and other defences of repressed energy that we build up. Often, we automatically find that our relationships—with friends, family, workmates, or even complete strangers—become clearer, more honest, and more straightforward. When we stop expending energy to keep up the façade of pretending to be someone we are not, we can start to use all of our energy to enjoy being ourselves.

However, just because we have learned to sort ourselves out, it doesn't mean that everyone else has. Until the world becomes full of enlightened energy-workers, we will have to keep dealing with other people's stuck stuff.

You know the kind of people I'm talking about. You feel your spirits dip when they walk up to you. You find you are exhausted after just a few moments of talking to them. They seem to be psychic vampires, sucking out all your vitality. Some can be just sheer unpleasant—nasty bullies, emotional blackmailers, manipulative, and sly individuals.

Before you do anything else, feel pity for them. You know just how unpleasant it feels to be loaded down with heavy stuck energy. How do you think they feel? One of the strongest techniques you can use is also the most simple. It entails sending pure loving energy to the person who is causing you grief. You can do this from anywhere without the person knowing.

1   Center yourself and focus on your breathing.

2   Direct your awareness to your heart chakra—feel the chakra spinning steadily.

3   Imagine a pure golden-white stream of divine universal energy shooting through your crown chakra and down into your heart. The whole chakra becomes full to bursting with this wonderful, loving, pure energy.

4   Send it out to the difficult person. Imagine it hitting them in the heart chakra and infusing their body with love and light. Be careful not to play games with this. Just send the loving energy—don't try to be clever or send wishes for them to be nice to you!

That's it. I used this regularly on a very difficult boss I ever had. Whenever she would burst in furiously, I would sit quietly and direct loving energy to her. It was tough, but it did work. She could tell something was happening because she would look at me suspiciously. "What are you doing to me?" she would ask.

SHIELDING TECHNIQUES

While the previous technique is very useful for people you know and have to deal with on a day-to-day basis, there are other methods that are more effective when dealing with strangers. Sometimes, you just need to protect yourself. The classic shielding technique is the energy bubble. I've come across this, or a form of it, in virtually every tradition under the sun. It is very simple, effective, and can be used anywhere. This is my version:

1 Breathe into your solar plexus and feel that chakra, strong and responsive, centering you. Breathe into your base chakra and feel the power of that chakra, rooting you to the earth. Breathe into your third-eye chakra, feeling that chakra respond with clear vision and foresight. As the chakras link up, it feels as though a rod of pure light is supporting your backbone.

2 Now, pull in pure energy from the universe through your crown chakra. Bring the energy down to your solar plexus and from there, let it burst out around you into a bubble of pure brilliant light, which surrounds your body totally, like a balloon.

3 Know that no negative energy can enter this powerful protective bubble—you are completely safe.

There are variations on this. I find the bubble the most effective for generally nerve-wracking situations or when dealing with people with whom I am uncomfortable. If, however, you feel someone is deliberately targeting you with negative energy, you might like to go one step further.

1   Follow Step 1 of the bubble technique—linking in with the chakras and pulling down the energy.

2   Next, send the energy out into the shape of a large box, with outward-facing sides that are mirrors—so the negative energy will bounce straight back to the person who sent it.

3   Once you have "disarmed" them this way, it could be the time to send that loving energy we have talked about (if you are feeling particularly philanthropic).

GUARDIANS
AND ALLIES

✦

Despite the huge cynicism, agnosticism, and atheism of this confused time, many people do have a strong sense of faith—if not in a particular religion, then in the form of a deep-rooted spirituality. You may feel you have a particular guardian or guardians—whether angels, gods, goddesses, spirits, ancestors, or animal allies. If so, by all means call on them for help during your energy-shielding exercises. You could have the four archangels guarding your bubble—or infuse the bubble with the symbol for Om or an image of the Buddha. Or reverberate a holy name or mantra through the bubble.

I work a lot with power animals—simply because they resonate for me and formed part of my shamanic trainings. I use this simple visualization to call on their energy whenever I need an energetic boost—when I have to go on a long journey, give a presentation, or have an important meeting. It's very comforting and surprisingly energizing. You may like to try it:

1   Stand upright and breathe into your solar plexus.

2   Feel your feet, firmly on the ground, connecting with Mother Earth. Remember your roots, which keep you steady and true. You are a child of the Earth.

3   Feel your head reaching upwards, connecting with Father Sky. Your feet may be rooted to the Earth, but your aspirations reach to the sky and the universe beyond. You are also a child of the heavens.

4   Now, before you, rises up the great animal spirit of the Eagle. A huge powerful eagle turns and looks at you with his glimmering, all-seeing eyes. You nod your head in acknowledgment and thanks. The eagle turns and spreads his wings. Now, you will see through Eagle's eyes, enjoying his sharp far-sighted vision.

5 Behind you rears up another huge figure—this time a great Grizzly Bear. You turn and look up into her deep eyes, noticing her sharp claws and her vast weight and strength. She is fiercely protective—who better to guard your back? Thank Bear and turn back, secure with her powerful presence behind you.

6 You hear a sniff to your right, trying to attract your attention. It's coyote, with his bright eyes dancing, tongue lolling out as if he were laughing. Coyote is a quick talker, smart, and a born negotiator. He can help you in any tricky situation. Be wary though—he's also a trickster. Don't let yourself become too clever for your own good or Coyote's strength becomes a weakness.

7 Finally, you feel a warm, sweet breath on your left arm. Turn and look into the dark melting eyes of Buffalo. She stands four-square, solid, and dependable. Buffalo will help to offset tricky coyote, keeping you grounded and stable.

8 Spend a moment feeling these great guardians all around you. Now you can walk into any situation feeling protected and powerful. Remember, at the end of the meeting or day to thank your guardians— it's traditional to offer a prayer and a pinch of tobacco or cornmeal.

CREATING ENERGETIC RAPPORT

✳

Of course, we don't always need to keep people at arm's length. Sometimes, we want to do exactly the opposite—to bring them closer, to create rapport.

There are two basic bonding exercises. One is for situations where two of you are knowingly working together, and the other is for when you are working without the other person knowing. Whenever you possibly can, always try the former. However, there are occasions where such an honest energy exchange isn't permissible (for example, in many business meetings); there are also some people who aren't quite ready on a conscious level to admit to something as bizarre as energy transfer. On a subconscious level however, they may be more than willing. The solo exercise can work with the permission of their energetic body, without blowing their conscious mind.

SOLO EXERCISE

1 Center yourself, breathing into your heart chakra.

2 Bring down loving energy from the crown chakra into the heart chakra and feel your heart fill with love, respect, and care for the other person.

3 Become clear about what you want to achieve. Don't try to change them—just open up the communication channels so you can have a more direct, honest interaction.

4 Send out a question to their heart chakra. Are they willing to receive your energy? Listen to your intuition.

5 If the answer is "Yes", then gently send out a golden-pink stream of loving energy from your heart chakra to theirs. Imagine that, in return, they send the same back to you.

6 Send a word of thanks to the universal source of all energy for allowing this exchange.

JOINT EXERCISE

1 Sit / stand opposite each other. Center yourselves, breathing into your heart chakras.

2 Bring down loving energy from the crown chakra into the heart chakra and feel your heart fill with love, respect, and care for the other person.

3 Send the energy out into a bubble surrounding the two of you. The two energies merge, becoming stronger as a consequence. Realize, with wonder, that the two together are stronger than two apart.

4 Now, if you wish, link yourselves at the various chakras. This can be powerful so, until you are totally sure of the other person, I would recommend you leave your energies merging at the bubble stage. If you want to, however, link at whichever chakras seem appropriate.

5 Be respectful of each other's energy. Do not barge in—ask for permission at each chakra.

SEXUAL ENERGY

CHAPTER SEVEN

Most sex talk focuses on the pure mechanics of sexual activity. It doesn't recognize sex for what it really is—an incredible energy exchange, and a force for both emotional and spiritual revitalization. In the East, the art of lovemaking has been recognized for creating sacred energy for many thousands of years. In India, Tibet, and China (to name a few) sex is taken very seriously. It is approached with a deep sense of awe and respect. In teachings such as Tantra, it is considered sacred; a form of divine worship.

Tantra is a form of yoga, said to have been practiced for over 6,000 years. While other forms of yoga employed physical training or meditation to reach unity with the divine, Tantra used everything in life—from washing the dishes to walking in the park (and, yes, sex) —it's the ultimate mindfulness. Tantra is technically a religion of sensuality—its church is the bedroom; its altar is your partner's body; its sacrament is sex. Tantric sex can give a swift, direct path to spiritual unity.

The theory is that the universe was once blissfully united, and whole. In Tantric mythology, this was symbolized by the endless joyous intercourse of the female and male divinities: the goddess Shakti and the god Shiva. Then the universe split into two. Shakti and Shiva were separated and creation became divided into positive and negative energies, light and darkness, male and female. So, now we suffer the pain of separation and it is this loneliness which apparently causes the sorrow and suffering in the world. Subconsciously, we still remember a fragment of the bliss of union and constantly yearn to be back in that innocent state of primordial harmony, of togetherness. Hence, the ultimate aim of Tantra is to reproduce that original divine union on a human scale—to become one (only for a short time) with the divine. Tantra teaches us to merge ecstatically with our partner and, through him or her, with the rest of the world.

Tantra can be a wonderful way to understand your body, your emotions, and your energy. However, if you decide you want to explore Tantra further in a group setting, be cautious. Some Tantric leaders abuse their position. A good Tantra teacher will insist that you are totally clear about your boundaries and that the work remains within those boundaries.

BRINGING SACRED SEXUALITY
INTO EVERYDAY LIFE

✳

1   You will need a full-length mirror and some candles.
    The room should be warm enough for you to feel
    comfortable naked.

2   Light the candles around the mirror and dim the lights.
    You can burn incense or aromatherapy oils (geranium,
    lavender, ylang-ylang, or sandalwood).

3   Undress and stand in front of the mirror. Look at your
    body, resisting the urge to criticize. Instead of focusing on
    the bits you dislike, find a part you like. Your first thought
    might be that you dislike all of it... But is that really true?
    Do you hate your fingers? Your wrists? Your earlobes?
    Your nostrils? Even if there is just one tiny bit which is
    okay, focus on that.

4   Think of the job it does—how wonderfully clever your
    fingers are, so dexterous and agile; how miraculous your
    hearing is, etc.

5   You may want to sit and really look at your genitals,
    without judgment.

6   Just be, quietly, with your body—for a good 20 minutes,
    if you can.

This may be hard yet persist. You may start to realize just how tough we
are on our bodies. You might even start to like your body, to appreciate it.
Do it whenever you can to increase your appreciation of how wonderful
you are. Always find something new that you like.

CULTIVATING
SENSUALITY

✳

Sensuality is the art of feeling energy through the skin. It's a delicious art and one we often ignore. Our skin is incredibly sensitive and, with a little gentle training, can become even more sensitive. Begin your exploration by noticing how different temperatures and textures feel on your skin. Lie naked on different surfaces—feel, really feel, how wood feels; how carpet feels; how wool feels different from leather or suede. Experiment with velvet, silk, fur (real on a cat; fake on a throw—what's the difference?). Can you detect the energy of the different materials? Does the real wood feel different from the synthetic rug? How does stone feel different to vinyl? Extend your senses—become more consciously aware.

When you have explored your home with your senses on full alert, go outside and do the same. Take off as many clothes as you can and lie on the grass, on the sand or pebbles of the beach, or on the leaves of the forest. Explore water—feeling the difference between the energy of the sea and that of a lake; between a swimming pool and a fast-running stream.

As you focus on feeling through your skin, you may be surprised by what you learn. With your newfound sensitivity explore what your body really wants. Does it prefer a firm touch or a gentle one? If you are lucky enough to live in an area where there are a variety of bodyworkers and can afford to have a massage, try out different forms. See whether you prefer the soft shimmering of Tragerwork or the strong stretching of Thai massage. What does each do for your energy?

PLAYING WITH
SENSUAL ENERGY

*

If you have a partner, now is the time to start working with each other. Before you launch into sex, spend time building trust and playing with each other's energy. Start with these simple exercises.

CONNECTING WITH THE BREATH

1   Sit down in front of each other, in whatever position feels comfortable.

2   Focus on your breathing. Keep your eyes cast down into your lap.

3   When you both feel centered, raise your eyes, and gently make eye contact. Don't stare and don't feel like you can't break eye contact. Just really look at each other.

4   How is your partner breathing? Slower or faster than you? Make a slight shift so you come more in tune. Your partner will be doing the same in response to you, so settle into a form which is halfway between the two of you. Don't force it and don't make yourself uncomfortable. Just see if there is a breath which suits both of you. How does it feel to share the same breath?

5   Now, gently hold hands. Imagine the energy flowing in and around the two of you. Experiment by holding up your hands, palms facing each other—about two inches apart. You may feel a pull, as if you two were magnets. Try moving your hands further apart and then closer together. How does the energy change?

This exercise is wonderful for building rapport and trust between you. Practice it as often as you can.

THE SEESAW

This yoga exercise helps to build trust with your partner. It is also energizing and helps to mobilize the body.

1 Sit down facing your partner.

2 Both of you, stretch out your legs as wide as feels comfortable. Touch each other's toes so your legs form a diamond shape.

3 Reach out to clasp each other's hands or fingers. If you can reach, hold each other's wrists. You may need to bend your knees slightly in order to touch.

4 Start to gently sway forward and backwards—one partner leans back while the other bends forward.

5 Breathe—inhaling as you lean forward and exhaling as you lean back. Smile at each other.

6 After a few minutes, stop swaying and slowly separate your hands and bring your legs back together.

7 Now, sit back to back with your eyes closed, for a few moments. Once more, connect with each other's breath.

BACK BENDS

Again, this is a wonderful exercise in trust. You have to rely, quite literally, on your partner. The deep stretching also stimulates energy and makes your body more relaxed and flexible. Practice this with caution, especially if one person is much larger or heavier than the other. Check with your physician or osteopath/chiropractor if you have any back problems.

1 Sit down, back to back. You can either stretch your legs out in front of you or cross them—whichever feels most comfortable. Link your arms together.

2 One of you leans gently forward, pulling the other so that his or her back is stretched over yours. Keep the movement slow and even—don't jerk and don't stretch too far for the comfort of your partner. Then reverse the movement so the other is "stretched".

3 Continue stretching back and forward in a smooth rhythm. Make sure you are relaxing your whole body, then you will be able to stretch even deeper. Don't forget to breathe!

SENSUAL MASSAGE

※

Giving a massage fosters intimacy and gently stimulates your sensual energy. There are plenty of books and YouTube videos available that explain how to give a massage. You can also just follow your intuition, and listen to your partner's feedback. Be very respectful.

1 The room should be warm. Light candles and put on relaxing music. Maybe burn some sensual oil.

2 Make up your massage oil. Use 6 drops of either ylang-ylang or sandalwood oil in 4 teaspoons (15–20ml) of a base oil like sweet almond.

3 Start on the back with your thumbs on either side of the spine, fingers pointing towards the neck. Allow your hands to glide slowly up the body and around the shoulders. Draw your hands lightly down the side of the back to your starting position. You don't have to be an expert—just keep a steady rhythm with the right amount of pressure for your partner.

4 Fleshy areas like hips and thighs can be kneaded gently: lift, squeeze, and roll the skin between the thumb, and fingers of one hand and glide it toward the other hand.

5 Curl your fingers into loose fists, keeping your fingers (but not the knuckles) against the skin. Work all over the body.

6 Make small, circling movements on the shoulders, palms of the hands, soles of the feet, and chest.

7 Form your hands into cup shapes and with quick movements, move over the skin, as if beating a drum. .

8 Ask your partner to turn over. Stroke the inner thighs; gently trace your fingers over the belly. Circle the nipples. Be teasing—gently touch the genitals as if by accident.

9 Be inventive. Towards the end, you could use your whole body to massage your partner, or trail your hair over them.

10 Put your hands into loose fists, and lightly bounce the side of the hands alternatively against the skin.

SACRED
SEXUALITY

✦

This is the point where we move from sensuality to sexuality. Mindful sacred sex can be quite confrontational so don't be surprised if it brings up tough emotions. Many of us have become adept at divorcing ourselves from our bodies, particularly during sex (however odd that sounds). Our society hasn't been at ease with sexuality for years, and generations have been brought up to think of sex as something smutty or shameful.

Take a few moments to ask yourself the following:

How were you brought up to think about sex?

———

Was it openly discussed in your household—or was it kept quiet and secret?

———

What were your early experiences? When did you first masturbate? How did you feel?

———

Did you and your friends or siblings experiment with yourselves and each other?

———

Did you see or hear any adults having sex? How did that make you feel?

Do you remember your first kiss? Your first sexual encounter? How was it and how did you feel?

———

Think about your sexual relationships? Have they been similar in any ways? Are you happy with your sex life? Your sexuality?

———

Is there anything you do in bed you don't feel happy with? What do you like? What would you change?

Ask your partner these questions too. Discuss them together. They can form the basis for an honest, open, and enlightening conversation. You might find that neither of you is happy with your sex life ,but you both thought the other was okay. You may find you have more in common than you thought. Sex is something we rarely discuss, even with our sexual partners. Try to break that taboo—it can be very healing.

Use your newfound knowledge to shift your lovemaking. Start by becoming more aware. Explore your bodies as if you had never seen them before. Notice everything, from earlobes to little toes.

Don't just pounce on each other, take it slowly. Use your freshly awakened sensual energy to detect the nuances of skin touching skin. Feel the texture of your partner's body. Use your hair, your nails, your eyelashes (yes, really) to stroke his or her body.

Find out what each of you loves. If you're not sure, ask. It always amazes me that in this ever more discriminating age, where you can spend five minutes just ordering precisely the kind of coffee you want, we accept whatever we're given in bed. I'm not suggesting you give orders—but you can guide your partner.

Rediscover the lost art of kissing. When you're an adolescent, there is nothing more mysterious and arcane than snogging, yet when we grow up, kissing often gets passed over. Try every kind of kiss you can imagine, wherever you can imagine. In Tantra, kissing is said to activate the chakras. You could move down the body, kissing each chakra—starting with the crown (that pure, spiritual benedictory kiss on the top of the head) and moving down to the base with a lusty smacker on the genitals.

ANIMAL
SEXUALITY

———————————— ✦ ————————————

Imagine if your sexual energy could express itself as an animal. What animal would it be? Would you be a slinky panther, a sinuous snake, or a playful chimpanzee? Act out your animal's energy and see if your partner can guess what you are. You might be two of a pair, or you might have very different animals. Take it in turns and tune in to the animal energy of your partner, as well as your own. Make love as though you were those animals—keeping within what feels good for your partner as well as you. Let go and become that animal, borrow its movements, its noises, its expressions. Or, be more subtle and make love with the energy of that animal. You can have a lot of fun with this exercise and it can be very liberating as animals don't have our sexual hang-ups or taboos.

UNCOVERING THE WILD WITHIN

In every ancient culture, there are gods and goddesses who are considered "wild", untamed, unfettered, and free. Their energy is primal, raw, and frequently sexual in nature. Sexual energy, as we've seen in the base chakra, is one of our earliest, most basic needs.

There is a lot of humor portrayed by these entities too. Baubo, the strange little Greek goddess, has eyes in her breasts and her mouth is in her vulva. She tells bawdy stories and ribald jokes. Then, there's Pan, the priapic god with the huge erect penis, which always leads him into trouble. Baubo and Pan's earthy sexuality is good medicine for us—they teach us not to take ourselves or sex too seriously. Most of the ancient male gods have powerful sexual energy. Whether you identify with Osiris or Zeus, Cernunnos or Shiva is a matter of personal preference. Many female goddesses are also sexually powerful and undoubtedly, women's sexuality has suffered during the past centuries. Modern women often need to rediscover their inner "wild woman", as discussed so eloquently by Clarissa Pinkola Estes in Women who Run With the Wolves. Read about the wild goddesses—Kali, Sekhmet, Medusa, and Erishkegal. Meditate on them and conjure their wildness into your sex play.

ELEMENTAL SEX

Make use of the natural elements within sex. It may sound like a cliché but try making love by a roaring fire. Pluck up your courage and have sex outdoors on top of a windy hill; in water (the sea, a lake, or stream); under the whispering branches of a tree. Feel the differing energies of fire, wind, water, and earth, and play with them. Imagine you are made of the earth, take on its steady, deep-throbbing energy; merge with its slow heartbeat. Touch each other softly, as lightly as the air itself. Be playful, like the wind, surprising, unpredictable. Then, feel fire energy, flickering over your body, scorching your lips, tingling your penis, your vulva, lapping like a small persistent tongue. As you become more aroused, feel the water energy mounting up within, rolling and thundering like huge breakers as it consumes your entire body in its embrace.

RAISING ENERGY WITH TANTRA

Aside from the mystical joining of male and female forces during lovemaking, Tantra aims to unite the male and female forces within their own bodies. In fact, some modern schools of Tantric yoga do not use physical sex at all but concentrate on this more esoteric union. The practice is called "Raising Kundalini".

Kundalini is the fire serpent that lies coiled in the base of the spine (or, some schools say, between the breasts of a woman and at the base of the spine in a man). It is the material manifestation of the divine female energy of the goddess Shakti. In most of us, Kundalini lies quietly slumbering, quite unaware that her divine counterpart Shiva is up in our head. Exercises involving visualization and rhythmic contraction of the anal sphincter are supposed to "wake" Kundalini who will then start to ascend through the chakras right up to the head where she joins in ecstatic union with Shiva. The result is a vast surge of energy and euphoria. However, most Tantric teachers say it is not advisable to attempt to wake Kundalini until you are quite far along the mystic path. So, I am not going to explain precisely how to raise Kundalini here. This is one area where it does seem as though people can progress too swiftly for their own good. If you practice the other exercises in this book, it is quite likely that you will automatically awaken the serpent power—in a totally safe and natural way.

ENVIRONMENTAL ENERGY

THE ENERGY
OF THE HOME

CHAPTER EIGHT

Homes have an energy of their own. In some, you will feel an immediate
sense of wellbeing and relaxation while others will make you feel harried
and unsettled. Some feel full of foreboding, as if they were filled with
unpleasant psychic energy. Once you understand the concept of vital
energy, these differences make sense. Just as we humans need to keep
our internal energy balanced, so does energy flow in buildings. Yet in the
West, hardly anyone knows how to shift energy, so we live in homes full
of ancient stagnant energy. The very fabric of our homes soaks up the
energy of the people who live in it—some very old houses could be full of
centuries of arguments and bad moods.

The aim of home energy is to be able to shift the mood of any room. You
can cleanse your place of any old unpleasant atmospheres and then
claim it as your own. This is particularly useful when you move into a new
home. The space will be full of the vibrations of the last inhabitants. You
need to move their energy on and install your own.

Of course, other wiser cultures have a long venerable tradition of
space clearing and cleansing—the Chinese system of feng shui, the
Indian vastu shastra, the Native American smudge ceremony, and the
Balinese bell-ringing and flower offering ceremonies. Let's try to reclaim
the lost art of energy sensing here in the West.

When you take the time to tune in to your home, you might gain
surprising insights. You could realize that you need more fun, more
peace, or more serenity in your life. You might gain a sudden inspiration
and "see" the perfect color to decorate your living room. Don't dismiss
these thoughts—maybe write them down in your journal and let them
settle. Come back after a few days and discover how you feel about them.
You might discover that your home held all the answers all along.

Before trying any energy shifting work in your home, you need to attune
yourself to the energy of your home as it stands. Prepare yourself by
taking off your shoes and any jewelery.

SENSING THE ENERGY
OF YOUR HOME

✦

1 Sit down quietly and bring your focus to your breath. Gently shut your eyes.

2 Connect with the chakras: feel the base chakra connecting you to the earth; the crown chakra linking you with the cosmic energy of the universe. Feel your solar plexus chakra, the center of your body, uniting the two.

3 Breathe into your solar plexus, feeling its strength and purpose radiating out through your body. Imagine that your energy is putting out feelers, gauging the energy of your home.

4 Let your solar plexus, your "gut reaction", tell you where the center of your home lies.

5 How does the energy feel in your home? What word would you use for the energy? If your home were to have a secret name, what would it be? Just see what pops into your head.

6 Go to the center of the home and honor the spot. Light a candle, burn some incense, and make contact with the energy. Ask your home what it would like from you—some places need psychic cleansing, some want a lighter, happier atmosphere, and some just want peace and quiet.

DECLUTTERING
AND CLEANSING

✦

You might notice that you need to have a clear out. There is nothing that upsets the smooth flowing of energy in the home as much as clutter. Energy flows most freely in smooth harmonious lines. Clutter provides an obstacle that blocks energy flow, so it becomes stuck, like dust in a corner. The stuck energy attracts more energy until you end up with a mound of clutter, surrounded by an ever increasing "pile" of stagnant energy. Next, things start to go wrong in your life—you may feel "stuck" and frustrated. Surely more than enough reasons to get clearing?

However, go carefully. I'm alarmed by the way decluttering has become almost a cult-like activity. Yes, it can be hugely liberating to clear our "stuff" (in all ways) but be mindful. Some "things" comfort and soothe us. The benefits of decluttering also depend on the type of person we are. So be kind to yourself and do what is right for you.

Have bags or boxes ready. One for absolute rubbish; one for things which belong to other people; one for things that can be sold, upcycled, or given to charity. Once you have sorted out your clutter, get rid of it immediately. Don't be tempted to keep it hanging around or it will sneak back.

Go through each room. First, clear the obvious mess and then look beyond it. Do you really need all those clothes? Do you really need every book cramming your bookshelves? Bookshelves should always have some gaps—to welcome new knowledge. Are you keeping things out of guilt— family heirlooms for example? The energy of the universe delights in free exchange. If you are miserly with things and hoard, you are telling the universe you don't need anything else. Allowing things to move away from you makes space for new things to flow into your life.

Now give your home a good spring clean. Open all the doors and windows and let in the fresh air. Scrub the floors. As you do, imagine you are scrubbing away all the old negative energy, leaving the place ready to welcome in the new positive vibrations.

CLEARING TECHNIQUES

Once your house is clean and clutter-free, you will have a clear space with which to work. Every ancient wisdom and culture has ceremonies and techniques for shifting energy. The following techniques come from a variety of sources. You can use them all or pick the ones that appeal to you. Of course, you are also free to shift or alter them as your intuition demands—a vital part of cultivating your own energy.

Before you start any of these exercises, spend some time readying yourself. Take a shower or have a bath—add a couple of drops of bergamot or lemon essential oil. Dress in clean comfortable clothes but leave your feet bare and don't wear a watch or any jewelery. Stand in the energetic center of your home and center yourself. The bubble of light exercise on page 94 is a useful way to cleanse your own energy in preparation. If you have any spirit guardians (guardian angels, or a power animal), you may like to ask for their help in this work.

CLAPPING

Work systematically around the room and clap into the entrance, the windows, the center and, above all, each corner (energy gets stuck in corners). At first, the sound may be dull but as you repeat your clapping, it should become clearer. Keep going until the sound becomes clear.

SAGE CLEANSING

Smudging comes from the Native American tradition. You can buy smudge sticks online or you can make your own. (These are bundles of sacred herbs— traditionally sagebrush, cedars, and sweetgrass). Bind together lengths of your chosen herbs and leave them until almost dry. Rosemary, lavender, and culinary sage make good alternatives. Light your stick and blow on it until it is smoking well (but not flaming). Fan the smoke around you to cleanse your own aura.

Then, send smoke into each corner of the room plus the center. Ask the sacred spirits of the plants to take away all negativity and replace it with beneficial healing energy. Make sure you thank the spirits when you have completed your work. If you are interested in taking this further, my book *The Smudging and Blessings Book* goes into more detail.

INCENSE

Incense can also cleanse energy in a similar way. Choose a scent you like (your intuition will guide you). You can direct the smoke as before or leave one burning in each room.

SOUND CLEANSING

Many cultures use bells, rattles, drums, and other sounds to cleanse the air. Center yourself and ask the spirit of each instrument to help you in your cleansing. Beat, rattle, or ring as you go around the home, imagining all the negativity being driven away by the sound. If you don't have an instrument, you can always use your own voice.

The chakra toning exercise on page 38 is very cleansing. Once you have cleared your own chakras, you can use it to direct sound out into the home. A house is like a body and it has chakras or energy centers, just as we do. So, resonate the base chakra into the foundations of your house; sound the crown chakra into the roof. Use your imagination and intuition to detect where the other chakras lie in your home. The kitchen might be the solar plexus—or it could be the heart of your home where everyone gathers. Where would the throat chakra be, as the center for communication? The front door perhaps—or the room with the desktop or landline?

FENG SHUI
AND VASTU SHASTRA

---　✳　---

In countries such as China and India, buildings were situated traditionally according to precise energetic rules. In China, the science of placement is known as feng shui, in India as vastu shastra—both offer very stringent guidelines about where one should build, and where one should not. They are complex sciences, based on many thousands of years of energy observation.

The theory in both systems is the same. When the energy of a house is well regulated and smooth running, the lives of the inhabitants will run smoothly too. There is not the space here to go into these disciplines in huge detail (my book Spirit of the Home will help further). However, there are certain things that anyone can do to get the energy moving smoothly, without the need for detailed knowledge of either system. Try these:

SIMPLE HOME ENERGIZERS
AND HARMONIZERS

USE AIR PURIFIERS

Air has an electric charge. Think how good you feel when by the ocean or out in the countryside where the air is negatively charged. Positive ions, which build up in houses and cities— particularly where the air is polluted, make us feel tired and irritable. Ionising air purifiers can help keep the air negatively charged and will swallow up dust and banish bad smells. If you don't like the idea, keep bowls of fresh water in rooms to absorb positive ions.

NAME YOUR SPACE

Naming your home gives it personality and links it to you energetically. Use your intuition to pick a name that suits you and your house. You may find it has two, or even more names: its "outer" name which it wears for the world, and its "secret" name which outlines its underlying energy.

USE THE POWER OF SCENT

Aromatherapy oils make a house feel brighter and more energetic— or can create an atmosphere of calm and tranquillity.

Try peppermint, or lemongrass for an uplifting effect, or sandalwood and lavender for relaxation. Geranium is cheering, while the citrus oils (lemon, orange, lime, grapefruit) are refreshing and uplifting. Use them particularly in kitchens and bathrooms.

ALLOW SOUND INTO YOUR HOME

Feng shui uses wind chimes as a cure for a host of problems. Even if you don't need them for a specific purpose, the soft sound of their chimes as the breeze moves them is lovely. Choose chimes with a sound you like (they vary enormously), and site them so that they will chime gently.

The sound of water is soothing and energizing too—indoor waterfalls can activate the energy in a room. Think about having an interesting water feature outside too. A small fountain makes a lovely spot for meditation—site it near to the house so you can hear its music from indoors. If you have young children you will need to choose carefully—pick one where the water is extremely shallow and runs over large pebbles or a boulder so that toddlers can't fall in.

HAVE LIFE IN YOUR HOUSE

Live creatures and plants bring energy into your home. If you work on-screen a lot, your best friend will be a spider plant, situated behind the screen. Spider plants soak up radiation and also ionize the air. Succulents do a great job too.

Animals introduce energy into houses—but you don't need to cope with a large dog or even a small cat. In feng shui, goldfish are valued very highly (ideally, have eight red fish and one black in your bowl or tank—and keep the water fresh with an aerator). They are another good way to activate qi.

CHOOSE WELL-CRAFTED PRODUCTS

Handmade crafts always trump mass-produced items in the energy stakes. Natural materials (wood, stone, ceramic, metal, cotton, linen, wool) have energy while synthetics are energetically "dead". Choose items that please your soul and these "energy" objects will infuse your home with vibrant soulful energy.

FILL YOUR HOME WITH FLOWERS

Fresh flowers bring a wonderful energy into the home. You don't have to spend a fortune on expensive shop-bought bouquets—branches in bud or bloom look wonderful. Pick armfuls of "weeds", or grasses. Grow wheatgrass—it looks fabulous, and can be added to juices and smoothies for an energy hit. Or reclaim your childhood by growing cress on blotting paper. Sprinkle the seeds in the shape of your initial—or be really clever and make a mandala or the Om sign for a mystical living plant display.

BRINGING COLOR
INTO YOUR HOME

───────────────────── ✳ ─────────────────────

One of the simplest ways of changing the energy in your home is to use color. You don't need to redecorate—you can introduce splashes of color to energize particular corners of your home. A feng shui consultant or Vedic astrologer would take into account your individual birthdate before choosing specific healing colors. However, you can experiment yourself. Look at your space—do any colors actively jar?

Think also in terms of the chakras. Vibrant reds and oranges relate to the lower chakras and work best in downstairs rooms. Yellow is a good downstairs color that can also be an intermediary between the levels, but use only soft hues upstairs. Green bridges two floors and works everywhere. Blues are great for bedrooms and bathrooms. Violets and soft indigos are fine for bedrooms and even better for top-floor meditation or relaxation rooms.

BALANCING THE ENERGY OF
YOUR HOME WITH THE ELEMENTS

If your home were an element, which would it be? Do you live in a passionate fire home or a cool cerebral air home? Is yours an emotional water home or a practical, down-to-earth earth home? You can often tell by the colors to which you are drawn—earthy homes are usually filled with muted browns, splashes of terracotta, and brick red. Fire homes are bright and vivid. Watery homes are filled with soft, flowing shades of the sea and the riverbed: they are often artistic homes but can be cluttered. Air homes are clean, airy, spacious, often minimalist, and slightly cool. Your home could be a combination of any or all of these—in which case you probably lead a pretty balanced life. If you fall solely into one category it may be worth introducing some other elements too. Once you start to play with elemental energy, all kinds of interesting things could come into your life: new possibilities, fresh opportunities, maybe even new relationships (or breakthroughs in existing ones) could emerge.

FIRE – THE ENERGIZER

Fire has been used to bring energy, spirit, and soul to the home in every culture since the beginning of humankind. The original heart of every home was the hearth, the living flame—in the past, it was honored as a deity in its own right. When a young woman married, her mother would bring fire from her own hearth to that of her daughter's. The young woman would then become mistress of her own home, and guardian of its energy.

Fire will usher fresh vibrant energy into the house. There is nothing more comforting than gathering around a real fire in the chill of winter. Gaze into its depths and see if you can see the flickering salamanders—the spirits of fire.

If a real fire isn't possible, bring the fire element into your home with candles. Candle magic is ancient, simple, yet very effective.

Choose a color that suits your purpose. Blue will help you achieve peacefulness and balance; red or yellow colors will bring lively energy. If you are seeking love or

wish to conceive a child, burn a pink candle in your bedroom. A green candle is helpful for money and abundance. Yellow candles bring joy and conviviality and also help with concentration. Focus your intention—why are you lighting the candle? Concentrate intensely while lighting it. You could also write your wish on the candle and watch your intent burn, sending your desire up into the ether, where it can be made manifest.

Hanging cut-lead crystals in windows brings in the fire energy of the sun. Hang mirrors in strategic places so that the sunshine can be reflected into the home.

WATER – THE PURIFIER

Water has been used in spiritual ceremonies since ancient times, and it's very important in modern baptist services. After an argument, the air in a room might seem thick and almost charged with negative energy. The fastest way to neutralize this residual energy is to mist the room. The fine spray also creates an environment that is rich in negative ions—the kind you find next to a waterfall, by the sea, or in a pine forest. Use spring water and lightly spray all over the room.

You can also use the Bach flower remedies in a mister — maybe Rescue Remedy after an argument or illness; Cherry Plum for calm, quiet courage; Star of Bethlehem to clear tension; Water Violet for tranquillity, poise, and grace. Equally, you could try adding a drop (no more) of essential oil to the misting water. Use lemon or grapefruit in the kitchen; geranium or bergamot in the living room, and lavender or sandalwood in the bedroom.

AIR – THE TRANSFORMER

While water heals, cleanses, and rejuvenates, the element of air transforms. Our bodies react emotionally and powerfully to different scents, and the smells in your home can contribute to or detract greatly from the way you feel about it. A simple way to enliven a room is to light a stick of incense. Choose a scent that you like, which feels appropriate for the room. Aromatherapy can also be powerful medicine for the home; though be careful with essential oils if you are pregnant or suffer from epilepsy and consult an aromatherapist before using them.

Bring fresh air into the house whenever you can—open the windows every day—if only for a few minutes. Fans circulate air (the old-fashioned ceiling fans look great too). Air-conditioning, unfortunately, can actually have the opposite effect and can de-energize the home. If you have to use air-conditioning, keep it on as little as possible.

A sense of air comes through a feeling of having the space to breathe as well. Try to have at least one room in the house which has an airy quality—without too much furniture: a room of possibilities, where your mind is free to roam unfettered. Such rooms are wonderful for children too as they can move about more freely, in the wild way they often need.

EARTH – THE STRENGTHENER

Earth is grounding and strengthening. It brings stability, ancient wisdom, and power into our lives. We all need a sense of earth in our homes, particularly when living in apartments without firm foundations beneath our feet. Nowadays, when we live so much in our heads or "in the ether", we need to make sure we keep our feet firmly on the good sweet earth.

Salt provides one of the most powerful ways of bringing earth energy into the home. It has the ability to neutralize negativity and cleanse the aura. It has been used in rituals for centuries: in the past, church bells were anointed with salt and water to bless them. An ancient baptist ritual saw the baby rubbed with salt to repel demons. We still throw a pinch of salt over our shoulders to "hit the devil in the eye". If ever you feel as if you are being thrown off balance by outside influences in your life, try the following. Take salt and make a large ring around the periphery of your room, including all the corners. Then, make a smaller circle of salt right around your bed. Just a small trickle will be effective.

Crystals and semi-precious stones help to bring the earth element into your home, acting as catalysts and transformers for energy. You will undoubtedly know "your" stone—it's the one which calls your name.

Dedicate a stone as your "home" crystal. Simply perform the chakra balancing technique (see page 31), then visualize pure energy coming down through your crown chakra into your heart chakra and from there into the crystal you are holding in your hands. Be clear about your intent—for example, the stone could be to protect the space, to bring in warm loving energy, to guard a child's room, or to foster good relationships.

NATURAL ENERGY

CHAPTER NINE

How does the energy of a stone differ from that of a piece of wood? What does the river say as it flows past? Where are the secret shrines of the Earth Spirit? Few of us know any more. We have become divorced from the natural world, from its ever shifting, fluctuating energy. We hide away in our air-conditioned or centrally heated homes and rarely feel the cold breath of the north wind and the scorching heat of the noonday sun. When we do go out, we still keep ourselves apart from nature: we park our cars in picnic spots and sit on benches or portable chairs. If we go to the beach, we lie on rugs. Rarely do we feel the grass or stone or sand under our feet. Rarely do we feel the wind in our hair or the rain on our skin.

What fools we are. Despite our attempts at taming it, it is still a beautiful world. Think of the dappled green of a forest with shafts of sunlight glancing through the trees. Summon up the rainbow shimmering through a waterfall. Remember the awesome power of the mountains; the heaving vastness of the sea. Visualize smaller beauties too: a fresh new bud, full and sticky; a butterfly alighting gently on a flower; a young puppy bounding with the sheer joy of life.

Our ancestors would have laughed at the idea of us having to search for the energy of the natural world. To them, the world was their soul, just as they were the soul of the world—there was no distinction. Then came civilization and an awareness that on the one hand stood us humans, while on the other hand—out there, apart from us—stood the world, foreign and dangerous. Our perspective changed: instead of feeling ourselves to be part of the natural world, we came to view ourselves as outside the natural world, above the natural world. Nature and its resources began to serve us, to be moulded to our needs and desires. Worse still, we began to almost "punish" Nature and put her "in her place", to show our dominance and our superiority.

It is as if we have been trying to deny that, for all our intelligence and material wealth, we are creatures like any others—we are born, we live and we die, according to Nature's rule and to the spinning of the thread.

RECONNECTING
WITH EARTH ENERGY

If we want to reclaim our birthright as energy beings, we have to do something to close the huge rift between us and the rest of nature. The only true way to heal this rift is to accept, truly, that we are part of the great cycle of Nature—no more or less than the other denizens with whom we share this planet. When we are cast adrift from earth energy, we remain dimly aware that something intrinsic is missing in our lives. We need to start, in the smallest of ways, to sense the whole world "out there". Try looking at everything—the grass, an insect, the earth—as if seeing it for the very first time. Don't just use your sight—use your other senses too. Listen to the sounds of nature—even in the heart of a city you can still hear the rustle of trees, the bird-song, and the trickle of water. Go out and touch the bark of a tree, stroke a leaf, or plunge your hands into the soil. Begin to be more aware of the world outside our houses, offices, and cars. Start, just start, to think of yourself as part of this great cycle of life.

STONE AND LEAF ENERGY

Let's start small. Pick up a stone and a leaf—any stone and leaf will do.

1 Feel the weight and texture of the stone; its coolness. Sense its age. Imagine what it has quietly witnessed. How would it feel to be that stone? What is "stone energy" like? Try to feel its rhythm.

2 When you feel you know your stone, place it to one side and pick up the leaf instead. Feel and smell the difference.

3 Trace the veins of your leaf. How would it feel to be a leaf, delicate yet attached to the strength and flexibility of a tree? To have the sun falling on you: the sun convert you to energy and food? Imagine the leaf's life cycle—concentrated as a bud, slowly pushing out into the sunlight, unfurling, growing, and spreading; then fading, drying, and dying. Falling to the ground and returning to the earth. The cycle is quite different to that of the stone. Keep the stone and leaf with you—perhaps on a desk or in a drawer.

LISTENING TO EARTH ENERGY

Another way of learning how to connect to earth energy is to Listen (with a capital L). This is so simple it sounds like child's play (and it is— I learned this approach as a Girl Guide), but don't dismiss it for that. Some of the greatest lessons we could learn are taught in kindergarten or at Scout camp.

1   Find somewhere you can sit out in nature, undisturbed. It could be in a field, a wood, on a beach, up a hill, in a garden, or park. Sit on the ground and make yourself comfortable. You need to give yourself at least 20 minutes.

2   Close your eyes softly, and bring your attention to the breath. Now turn your attention to the world outside and start to listen. Just listen… really listen.

3   Before long, you'll start to tune in to the complex hum of nature: the bewildering array of bird calls; the scurrying of insects busying around; the movement of leaves; the tentative progress of small creatures nosing through the undergrowth. As your hearing becomes more refined, you will hear still more: a leaf dropping to the ground; a bud opening; the hum of the earth itself. That's when you begin to Listen (with that emphatic capital L).

4   If your thoughts wander off, gently pull them back.

5   Time may become fluid—you might not be sure whether you have been listening for a few minutes or several hours. If you feel nervous sitting alone, ask a friend to come with you or to call you back after 20 minutes.

6   Write down what you heard and how you felt. Explore the feelings that came up.

THE
SHAMANIC PATH

There are people who can guide us back to living with earth energy. The indigenous peoples, who have never lost connection with the earth, can teach us lessons in finding our soul in the land. Chief Seattle, the Suquamish and Duwamish leader put it beautifully:

"Whatever befalls the earth befalls the sons and daughters of the earth. We did not weave the web of life; we are merely a strand in it. What we do to the web, we do to ourselves."

Spiders are ancient creatures and in many cultures, a Spider Goddess was said to have created the entire world. Shamans say that the Spider weaves the web of Wyrd, or fate—an energy web that spreads all over the world, and out through the universe. We are all part of the web; what affects one part of the web will reverberate and affect everything else.

The idea of sacred earth energy was once prevalent all over the world. The earth's vital energy was understood to flow in invisible energy channels, just as our life energy flows through our bodies. In Europe, we see vestiges of this belief in the ley lines and straight tracks; in the "fairy-ways", in the standing stones and the sacred wells.

Start to think of your connection to the whole world. Not just in relation to your tiny patch of turf, but to the entire earth. Next time you watch a documentary on some far-flung part of the world, remember that it is just another part of the web, your web. Don't disassociate yourself from the world—accept it. Broaden your outlook to embrace it. Become aware and knowledgeable. Know your web.

THE MEDICINE PATH

Shamans remain close to the energy of the land. They watch for patterns in the web, seeing everything that happens in the natural world as having meaning and resonance for our own personal energy field. Their training involves going out into nature alone with the hope of contacting the spirits and the energy of plants, animals, trees, and the earth itself.

You can bring this awareness into your own hikes and even everyday life. Start by becoming aware of the natural world. Look at the trees—are they blowing in a particular way? What message might that have for you? A bird might fly in front of your car—what is the bird and what might its flight mean? A large pebble might plant itself in front of you as you walk to work. What message could it bring? Follow your intuition. As you become more attuned, you will find that nature can offer you many answers and much wisdom—if you only watch, listen, and feel.

Most shamans develop special relationships with animals, birds, and plants. Some of these become '"allies", lending the shaman their particular energy or strengths. If you haven't already practiced this exercise on page 96 for contacting the four great spirit animals, perhaps now is the time.

SACRED
ENERGY

—————————— ✦ ——————————

Every land has its sacred places—from the great, mysterious, sacred sites
of antiquity, to quieter, more hidden spots that a stranger could easily
pass by. These places—whether a hill, a cave, a spring, or a structure built
or positioned by humans (such as a stone circle; a church or a soaring
menhir), all seem to draw the soul toward them like a magnet. They touch
us in deep and unfathomable ways. These are places where earth energy
runs particularly strong. Our ancestors marked them as sacred, often
believing they were the residing places of gods, goddesses, spirits, and
elemental forces. If we take the time to stop and use our senses, we can
often pick up on this. If you feel unsure about how to sense natural energy,
you might find it easier to go first to one of these "power" sources where
the energy runs strong and can be more easily detected.

As a child, I had many favorite sacred spots. They ranged from the
large "public" sites, such as Glastonbury Tor and the Cerne Giant to
tiny corners—a nook in a suburban wall where I left gifts of flowers and
stones. As I grew up and travelled, I discovered many more mysterious
and powerful sacred spaces, full of awesome earth energy. My soul
shrank at first from the huge vastness of the Mojave desert in southwest
USA. I felt like an ant—tiny and inconsequential. Then, I took a deep
breath and drank in the raw power and beauty of the place—and
absorbed the energy of rock and sky. I felt dizzy at the sight of the soaring
mountains and endless forests of Wyoming and New Hampshire; then
exhilarated by the clean, fresh air and the timeless splendour of every
tree and mountain. Later on, when visiting Egypt, stepping into the King's
Chamber of the Great Pyramid at Giza, was like being plugged directly
into a battery; a source of superhuman spiritual power. In France, the
ancient prehistoric cave paintings filled my soul with awe.

Yet strangely, when I think about the places that resonate the most, they
are smaller, more personal spaces. There is a particular spring, hidden
down a forgotten track, tucked away amid trees and curling ivy. It is
not large or spectacular in any way, but it holds magic. I approach it as
though visiting a lover, taking them something—a daisy chain; a tiny

posy of wild flowers tied with grass; a little figure whittled from wood. Suddenly, I'm there and I am overcome, once again, by its simple beauty. I sit on a rock and look into its bubbling waters. I give it my gift and watch it being swirled around gently in the ripples. I could stay for hours, listening to birdsongs, watching the water.

Of late, "my" spring has become better known and I have found litter by its banks, and been unsettled by shouting voices splitting its peace. With more visitors coming to the site, the local council has "tidied it up", replacing the old crumbling walls with safer new ones. The last time I went, I felt its spirit had almost vanished. Was the earth essence dying or was it just quietly moving on, away from the raucous voices and the disrespect? The same principle can be seen in many of the "great sites". Stonehenge has become almost like a creature in a zoo, to be ogled through the fences. The huge temples of Mexico, Egypt, and South America are swarmed over by hordes of tourists, only half listening to their guides as they bark out snippets of information.

What is the answer? Find your own sacred sites; discover your own special places. They lie in every neighborhood, whether rural, suburban, or entirely urban—it just takes a careful eye and an opening of your own energy to be drawn to them. When you do, make them yours. Approach them with reverence and always thank them for their restorative powers.

Visit the old sites, but mindfully and carefully. Pick up litter and take it away. Visit in the small hours—at twilight, at sunrise—when coach parties do not visit. Go alone or, if you are with others, be silent. Listen, watch, and feel. Allow yourself and the place enough time to get to know each other: sit softly and quietly; just be. Let us all get away from the continual, competitive race: the urge to notch up sites as if they were trophies. Come to learn. Quietly sit and wait for the place to communicate with you. It probably won't happen immediately; it may not happen at all. Shamans spend years building rapport with places. When, and if it does happen, you may find wonderful surprises.

SEASONAL
ENERGY

---------- ✳ ----------

Every month, every week, every day, every time of the day is different from the last and the one to come. Meander rather than march through the seasons. Take time to look at what's around you—the tiny miracles as well as the large extravaganzas of nature. Then, every so often, something truly incredible will reveal itself: two hares boxing in the early morning; a fawn curled in a cozy nest, with huge brown eyes staring; a cloudscape that looks like a series of floating islands in the reds and golds of the setting sun.

Take every opportunity you can to observe and participate in the wild world around us. You don't have to live in the heart of the country: a city changes too, by season and by the passing hours of the day. The changes may be more subtle, but there is still joy in catching them.

I remember clearly walking to school as a child. We lived in a London suburb and my walk took me along house lined roads, over a railway bridge and along the edge of playing fields. Every day, I saw something new, something wondrous. I was fascinated by tiny plants growing in walls, intrigued by the webs and cocoons built in hedges, moved by the shy wild flowers in odd patches of wasteland. Why lose that child's sense of wonder in the ordinary? Keep honing your senses to absorb the world around you. Allow yourself an extra five or ten minutes for every journey. It allows you time to look up to see the clouds and to look down at the ground. Even in city pavements, tenacious plants manage to break through the concrete. Mosses creep over walls. Insects are busy, going about their business.

Watch the changes as the weeks and seasons pass. As you become more sensitive, you might even find that your mood and energy are mirrored in some way by the rhythms of the natural world.

CITIES AND
THE WORKPLACE
CHAPTER TEN

There is energy in the city as well as in the natural world. It's a different
kind of energy, to be sure, but just as valid. If we want to be energy-
workers, we cannot divide up our lives—we should connect with all
the various forms of energy we find and work with them rather than
ignore them; we cannot focus only on the "spiritual", the "natural", and
the "good" energy. Many people divide their lives into compartments,
switching off as they leave home for work, and only switching on again
when they leave work to go home. Don't fall into the trap of thinking that
your daily work cannot be energy work—it most certainly can be. If you
invest your work with a knowledge of vital energy and if you connect fully
with the energy of your work and workplace, you will get far more out of
your working day.

Similarly, you can embrace the energy of the city. The movement of trains,
buses, cars, and bustling, frenzied people. Each shop and building has its
own energy, varying as much as that between a stone, and a leaf. Think of
a small, local independent store and compare it with a vast hypermarket.
Feel the difference in energy.

The energy of supermarkets and malls can be unsettling; it generally
moves very fast along long straight aisles and avenues, which is why
many of us feel uncomfortable in them. Spend a few moments grounding
yourself before you go into a supermarket. Focus on balancing your
chakras. Set up a bubble of protection to shield you from the harsh
energy that will be coming at you from all angles. Call on Buffalo's energy
to keep you earthed and grounded, solid, and balanced. Little things like
this can really help.

CITY
ENERGY

✳

City energy is exhilarating but it can also be exhausting. When you live in the city all the time, you become tuned in to its pace and get used to the constant bombardment of the senses. You build your own automatic psychic wall to protect yourself, until you learn to blank out the sound and sheer enormity of it all. You filter your daily experience. I spent the first thirty years of my life living in cities (in London and Manchester in the UK; near Boston in the US), and was totally at home in the urban environment. Nothing fazed me. When I moved out to the countryside, I found, within months, that I had lost my "city-wise" ways. When I returned to the city, everything was just too loud, too fast, and too much. I was out of step with the city energy. The key to dealing with city energy is to become an urban shaman. Take the lessons of the medicine path and apply them to the city.

SPACE DANCING

This exercise was taught to me by Sue Weston, a wonderful qigong, tai chi, and dance instructor. It's simple and useful. It tunes you in to city energy and gives you the personal space to be able to cope with it.

1   Become aware of the people around you as you walk. The aim is not to touch any of them. They will be walking blindly, but you turn ninja, walking silently through the forest, not making a twig bend or break.

2   You are "dancing" your way through the crowds, moving fluidly and smoothly, sliding through the hordes.

3   Anticipate how people will move; look ahead all the time; become aware of the whole space around you.

4   Let your vision flit from close distance to middle distance, and to far distance.

5   Send out your energetic feelers to sense where people are. In time you will find that you see "your" path through the crowd and the whole exercise will become supremely effortless.

ENERGY COMMUTING

There are two ways to deal with commuting or travelling in cramped conditions on public transport. You can choose to tune out the whole experience. Simply retreat inside your protective bubble and meditate. You can do this anywhere. If you are sitting down, just slump your head forward, everyone will simply think you are dozing. If you're standing up, sink into the qigong starting posture (page 70).

Alternatively, if you're feeling energetic and inquisitive, you could use your commuting time to test out your energy-sensing on other people. Practice aura detection (page 28) or gently probe into other people's energy fields. Ask permission (silently) and be willing to back off if you feel they do not want to "meet" you, on an energetic level. If you get the energetic go ahead, how does their energy feel? What can you learn from them? Is there anything you can give them in return? Maybe give them an "energy bath" by pulling down energy through the crown chakra into your heart chakra and then sending it out to their heart chakra, wishing them happiness, health, and peace. This is also good to do if you see someone looking harried, stressed, or in pain: perhaps a mother shouting at her kids or a homeless person begging on the streets. If you can't give financially, at least you can give energetically.

CITY MEDICINE

Walk mindfully through the city. Keep your senses awake for signs from the energy of the universe. There are birds in the city too—watch the flight of sparrows, blackbirds, thrushes, and wrens. You might see more surprising visitors too. I was once in a business meeting high up on the top floor of an office building. I was almost nodding off when one of my colleagues pointed out of the window: "Look, it's a kestrel," she said with amazement. We all watched the beautiful bird of prey with wonder—and returned to our meeting with a renewed sense of purpose.

Keep an eye out for the lessons of nature within the city. How can a tiny seedling push through the tarmac? Surely, only by gently, slowly, and surely, insistently making its way, never giving up, never thinking the odds are stacked against it. Now that's a message for modern life, isn't it? Or think about the way that a plant will bend and stretch itself to reach the light. We can be flexible too, learning how to move seamlessly, and perfectly adapting ourselves to find our ideal position. Just as birds make nests out of incongruous materials—so we can all look for gold amid the dross.

There are lessons to be learned from less natural things too. Listen to the rhythm of the train; watch the dance of the traffic; follow the lines of telegraph poles and electricity cables. See connections: ponder on these artificial forms of energy and how they work in our lives. Notice the buildings around you. Which work well and fit in with the energy of the city? Which seem out of place, ill thought out, or badly designed? Which have good energy, which attract bad energy?

CONSCIOUS MANIFESTATION

Once you start to tune into the energy of the city, you can have fun. One of the rules of energy-working is that when you give something your conscious attention, you send energy towards it. Hence, you start to manifest the so-called "law of attraction", which is the basis of all "magic", spells, and rituals. By paying attention and focusing your energy, you are affecting the energetic web that surrounds us. Energetic ripples spread out from you and—if you have focused your energy effectively enough, something will happen. Play with energy-work in a small way by manifesting parking places. Simply visualize, in perfect detail, where you want to park. See it clearly in your mind's eye; see the area around it, the cars around it. Then visualize a car leaving "your" space just as you drive up, or slightly before. See your car seamlessly entering the space. If you really focus, it works—truly it does. It's a technique I learned from a joke-shop "parking Buddha" figurine I bought years ago in Boston and stuck over the dashboard of my car. Yet, it's far from a joke when you're hunting for parking in the city.

Of course, you can use this technique for pretty much anything—such as to summon your bus or train when it's running late, or to manifest a seat when you're feeling weary.

OFFICE
ENERGY

✳

Nowadays, many of us work from home, which allows us more control over our environment (although this can still cause energy-related issues). However, the majority still work in offices and factories. Very few workspaces in the West have been built using energetic guidelines, and equally, few are built with employees' health and happiness in mind. Many are decorated using materials that outgas, emitting toxic fumes. Electrical equipment has an electromagnetic field that interferes with our own energy field, potentially making us feel off-color. Long corridors and large open plan offices with few windows make us feel insecure and harassed.

As if that were not enough, you are sharing space with all those other people with their worries, anxieties, hang-ups, and concerns. It's one giant energetic melting pot of disrupted energy—and often very uncomfortable.

THE
OFFICE SANCTUARY

✳

Just as you turned your home into a soothing sanctuary full of vibrant healing energy, you can also bring positive energy into your workplace. The rules are pretty much the same—whether you work from a corner of your living room or in a large shared office.

✴ Clear the clutter. Don't focus only on the physical clutter—take time every so often to give your digital files a spring-clean too.

✴ If you can, operate a clear desk policy: only have the thing you are actually working on right now on your desk. It makes good energy sense, as your energy will be focused on the one thing, rather than dissipated among several.

✴ According to feng shui, your desk should be positioned diagonally opposite the door, with you facing the door so you can see everyone who walks in. If this is impossible, have a mirror on your desk so you can see people approaching.

✴ If you work with someone difficult, place a crystal paperweight or a bowl of water on your desk. It will deflect any criticism or intolerance.

✴ Green plants are your lungs in an office. Certain plants can absorb negative energy and will thrive even in dark, dull places. Try peace lilies, spider plants, sansevieria, or succulents such as aloe vera.

✴ Invest in an air purifier and ionizer—it will make a big difference.

✴ Fresh flowers stimulate mental activity and cleanse the atmosphere. They are also a lovely reminder of the natural world and have a fresh, cheering energy.

✴ As I work from home, I have a candle burning while I work. It helps to focus the mind and brings the enlivening energy of fire. I also have an aromatherapy diffuser. If this isn't feasible, there are now many wonderful sprays and mists available that have a similar effect.

✴ Crystals are helpful allies. Clear quartz will amplify your energy; citrine will help to bring in money; turquoise is good for improving communication; garnets boost creativity; amethyst will help you have clear thoughts; obsidian is said to help with decision-making.

✴ Keep something on your desk that reminds you of your spiritual energy. I have a serene Buddha who reminds me to keep calm under stress and Shiva Nataraja to remind me to dance lightly through my working life.

OFFICE MAGIC

Your attitude and energy affect your work. If you feel negative and bored, it will be boring. If you consider your workmates dreary, they will drive you mad. Change your attitude and you will change your work. If you are stuck in a dead-end job, it's tempting to go through the motions. What a waste of your life. While you are looking for work that makes your soul sing, choose to love the work you do—however humble or humdrum. Simply invest it with energy—positive, vibrant humming energy.

Let me give you an example. I once worked in the box-office of a large exhibition center. When it got busy, I'd sit for eight hours a day in a kiosk, churning out tickets. It would have been so easy to switch off and work like a robot. Instead, my friend and I decided we would aim to connect, in a small way, with each and every customer. We felt completely energized and immersed in the challenge. The customers loved it too. We enjoyed an energy exchange with every person.

You can imbue any task with energy. If you are cleaning a floor, turn it into a meditation. Consider the act of cleaning to be a lesson in the transitory nature of life: you can change it, but only for a while.

If you deal with people on the phone, connect with them via your voice. If you work with numbers, look for patterns—the energy of the universe is apparently a numerical equation so working with mathematics or computer codes could be the most spiritual work of all. Look for lessons everywhere—keep an eye open for symbols, for meaningful coincidences, comments, and patterns.

I'm a huge believer in using oracular systems like the I Ching, the Tarot, and the runes. If you have a dilemma at work or want to know how to approach a problem or challenge, consult the oracle. Although the I Ching is the most challenging to master, I find it is also the most practical in its advice. If you cannot get to grips with the language of the original translation, there are now some excellent modern interpretations.

ENERGETIC MEETINGS

We can choose our friends but we generally cannot choose the people with whom we do business. Most difficulties come about because we have different viewpoints or kinds of energy. If you can bridge the gap between the points of difference, you are on the way to creating a more harmonious way of working. Don't fall into the blame trap of thinking, "It's his fault", "Well, if she won't make the effort ..." and so on. You have the power to influence the other person (in the nicest way possible).

✳ Make an energetic connection. Follow the technique on page 141. For most work-related energy-work, choose to connect at the solar plexus, heart, and throat. If your relationship needs grounding, use the base chakra. If you need to connect on an intuitive level, join at the third-eye chakra.

✳ In meetings, visualize the bubble of protection extending right around the table. Pull down energy through the crown chakra and send it into your heart chakra. Imagine the energy shooting out from your heart and connecting with everyone else, as if you were all spokes of a giant wheel; you all join together in the hub. It's a nice exercise to do if you work in a team.

✳ We often meet people with whom we don't gel. Imagine the other person is sitting opposite you. Now imagine you are sitting in their chair. If you were them, how would you answer? You can physically put another chair in front of you and swap positions if that's easier. Shift back and forward, asking questions, gaining insights. Don't leave until you understand how the other person feels and why. Use your new-found knowledge wisely.

✳ Bring playfulness, fun, and kindness into the workplace. Have a kind word for everyone; make an effort to give compliments and praise. Practice random acts of kindness. It may seem daft, but this "magical" approach is a powerful energy shifter.

SPIRITUAL
ENERGY

CONNECTING TO
SPIRITUAL ENERGY

CHAPTER ELEVEN

Are you wary of the word "spiritual"? Perhaps it reminds you of being dragged to church, synagogue, temple, or mosque when you were very young? Or perhaps it worries you because you're cynical about "fluffy angel and unicorn mumbo jumbo". Maybe, just maybe, you're scared of what might happen if you were to allow yourself to seek (and maybe find) the ultimate source of energy. Yet, if you have been following the path outlined in this book, you are already working with spiritual energy.

All energy is spiritual energy—whether we are referring to energy that runs through our bodies, that connects us with other people, that cascades through nature, or that hums in the city. Our body and mind are not separate from our soul. They are interconnected, each informing the other. It's how the energy is manifested that differs. W. E. Butler, the famous occultist, said: "See yourself not as a stranger in the universe, not even as a separate being apart from it, but as part of that living diversity in unity, and say...I am a Child of Earth, but my Race is from the Starry Heavens." (*Magic, Its Ritual Power and Purpose.*)

If you study the huge variety of religions around the world, all the teachings come down to the same thing. The universe is made up of energy. There is, if you like, one ultimate energy source to which we all belong: creation can be seen as a huge energy surge, which triggered a lightning flash of reactions. Pure spiritual energy from the source started moving down towards material manifestation. Gradually, it becomes denser, more capable of creating form. Eventually, it becomes solid enough to transform into matter. Our bodies and the physical form of the world around us are born. However, and this is very important, it is still the same energy in essence. We all have within us the divine spark of the original, ultimate energy source. That flame never dies and it can connect us back to our divine roots.

My preference when working with spiritual energy is to draw upon the vast wisdom and age-old tradition of the Kabbalah. It's something I came across when I was a teenager and have been studying ever since.

THE KABBALAH—
A MAP OF ENERGY

The Kabbalah offers a map of creation—from the first intention of "God" (the original source), down to the tiniest microorganism; it accounts for the swirling mass of energy and matter as well as the everyday anxieties that make up our individual psyches. Although the Kabbalah is Jewish in origin, it embraces all creeds and religions. The Kabbalistic world is one of opposites held in balance (similar to the concept of yin and yang).

Sadly, this ancient system was brought into disrepute in recent years when the Kabbalah Center hit international headlines with claims it was a cult. A follower won a sexual misconduct lawsuit and its celebrity fans faded away. However, let's be clear—this outcome relates to a particular group, not to the ancient tradition of Kabbalah itself. Just as I stressed caution when you are seeking a Tantra group, I would say the same when joining any spiritual center. People are fallible, even gurus are fallible (sometimes especially gurus). Follow your gut instinct. The exercises here are ones you can follow entirely on your own—with no need to join anything.

The Kabbalah explains that God created the world through divine speech; specifically using sounds that had numerical significance. These words created the sephiroth—ten spheres that map the energetic path from pure divinity down through various stages into the material world. You could say that the true language of the Kabbalah is mathematics. Certainly, the Kabbalah's descriptions of creation can be understood in terms of physics. By meditating on the spheres and paths of the Tree of Life, it is said that we can gain deep insights into our own nature, into our place in the world, and even into the nature of God.

The Kabbalah can be used in ways that are as simple or complex as you wish. Some people draw on the symbols of the Tree of Life as a source of meditation, to help them understand the different aspects of themselves or their lives. Others choose to study its teachings, poring over texts and debating the various attributes of the Tree of Life. Others see it as a true mystical path, offering a direct route to a closer experience of God.

THE TREE OF LIFE

The Tree of Life lies at the heart of the Kabbalah. It offers us a map of the conscious and unconscious, to the world around us, and to the many hidden energetic worlds that lie above and below our everyday consciousness. By meditating on each individual sephirah, or travelling the paths between the sephiroth (in a form of guided visualization called pathworking), it is possible to gain understanding of yourself and connect to the various forms of spiritual energy contained within the Tree.

Following are the basic attributes of the sephiroth. Can you see where some of the chakras might align with the Tree of Life?

MALKUTH—THE KINGDOM

Malkuth corresponds to the body and to the material, outer world—our universe. It is the lowest sephirah, the closest to our everyday life and hence, the starting point for all meditative work and journeys on the Tree. It represents the contact between our bodies and the world outside: how we relate to the physical world through our senses. The aim in Malkuth is to see a vision of our Holy Guardian Angel.

The main colors of Malkuth are yellow, olive, russet, and black flecked with gold. Its symbols include the equal-armed cross, a double cube, and the magic circle.

YESOD—THE FOUNDATION

Yesod embodies the subconscious: the energy we have picked up from our past and carry within us, often repressed and largely unknown. It also holds all of our future potential. Yesod is linked equally with our sexual nature and the Moon. The task of Yesod is to balance our selves, to make ourselves whole.

The colors of Yesod are indigo, violet, and very dark purple. Its symbols are perfumes and sandals.

HOD—GLORY

Hod is linked with the mind, the intellect, and our willpower. It is the sephirah of communication and its task is to learn true and honest communication, both between the various parts of yourself and with others. It is also the sphere linked to magic and spells—and with "mental" energy-work.

The colors of Hod are violet, purple, and orange. Its symbol is the apron.

NETZACH—VICTORY

Netzach is associated with feelings; both positive and negative energies such as love and hate, joy and sorrow. In Netzach, we learn to choose which emotions we experience, rather than be at their beck and call. Netzach is also linked with the creative arts—painting, dancing, and music.

The colors of Netzach are amber, emerald, and olive flecked with gold. Its symbols are the rose, the lamp, and the girdle.

TIPHARETH—BEAUTY

Tiphareth lies at the center of the Tree of Life. It represents the self, the soul, and pure self-awareness. The lesson of Tiphareth is to have a clearly defined sense of self that derives equally from thinking, feeling, and sensing. At this point, on the Tree, the task is to contact and converse with the Guardian Angel (linking yourself with a sense of the eternal, the spiritual).

Tiphareth's colors are rose-pink, yellow, and rich salmon-pink. Its symbols include the cross, the cube, and a truncated pyramid.

GEBURAH—SEVERITY

Geburah is the sephirah of judgment and unmitigated truth. It is linked with personal will and power. When balanced, this brings about strength, order, activity, and focused awareness. When out of balance, it can manifest in manipulation, selfishness, pride, overambition, and competitiveness. In this sephirah, one needs to be totally honest with oneself.

The colors of Geburah are orange, bright red, and scarlet. Its symbols include the pentagon, the sword, the spear, and the scourge.

CHESED—MERCY (SOMETIMES KNOWN AS LOVE)

Here we meet the manifestation of form—the "thought forms" of the mind. The challenge in Chesed is to balance the experience of love—to foster feelings of caring, sensitivity, and cooperation—without descending into dependence, attachment, the inability to say no, and wanting to please too much.

The colors of Chesed are deep violets, purples, and blues. Its symbols include the orb, the wand, and the sceptre.

DAATH—KNOWLEDGE

Daath is the one sephirah which is not situated on the Tree; it is a hidden sephirah that lies in the middle of the abyss, above Tiphareth and below Kether. Many see Daath in a negative light. It represents knowledge without understanding, restriction, and dispersion. It is also said to be the prime link to all that is evil and demonic in the world. However, translated into psychological terms, it could be said that the abyss holds the shadow, all the unresolved and irrational elements of the psyche, and that no one can cross the abyss into true spirituality without resolving these aspects.

As it is an invisible sephirah it has no color or symbols.

BINAH—UNDERSTANDING

In Binah, energy is just starting to turn into matter; it is the primal feminine force. Beneath it lies the abyss, the gulf between the actual world below and the potential world above. Binah is associated with spiritual awareness and love. Experiencing Binah is known as the "vision of sorrow"—on the one hand providing an understanding of the full impact of the "fall" into lack of connection; on the other hand, offering knowledge of the healing power of true grief.

The colors of Binah are primarily crimson, black, and dark brown. The symbols include the cup or chalice.

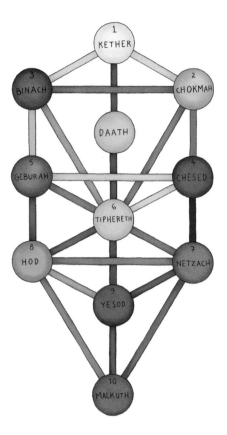

CHOCKMAH—WISDOM

Chockmah signifies spiritual will and purpose; the result of applying spiritual purpose to understanding. The experience is that of seeing God face to face. Chockmah represents the dynamic thrust and drive of spiritual energy—it is the primal masculine force.

The colors of Chockmah are primarily soft blues and greys and its symbols are all phallic: standing stones, the tower, and the rod of power.

KETHER—THE CROWN

Kether signifies the fount of creation, where life begins, where there is no distinction between male and female, energy and matter. No one alive can fully experience this sphere which represents union with God. However, it is said that one can glimpse the glory of God through this sephirah.

Kether is light. Its colors are pure white brilliance, and white flecked with gold; its main symbol is the equal-armed cross.

BUILDING THE
INNER TEMPLE

---　✳　---

Working with energy on this plane may awaken old forgotten feelings and cause repressed memories to emerge from our deep unconscious. It is sensible to do this energy-work within a safe container; a sacred space. Creating your own personal inner temple is also an important exercise in using your powers of visualization, which need to be strong for this work.

We go to church or to the mosque, the temple, the synagogue, or sacred grove because it can be much easier to connect with the spiritual in a place that is dedicated to the spirit. For the same reason, you will be building an inner sanctum, an energetic temple in which to work. It doesn't matter that your temple is in the imagination. Once you have learned how to build it, and have used it repeatedly, it will become as real to you on an energetic level as a physical building made of material bricks and mortar.

Your temple is just that—your temple. You can create it in a form that pleases you. If you have any religious affiliations, then you might want to build it on similar lines to the place where you worship or where you used to worship as a child (if that has pleasant memories). A temple can be a complex building, a simple room, or even a beautiful place in nature. Let's take a moment to think about what a sacred space means for you.

BUILDING YOUR INNER TEMPLE

1　Sit quietly and shut your eyes. Become aware of your breathing and bring focus to your heart chakra. Breathe into this chakra.

2　Imagine energy streaming from the universe down into the crown chakra, and into your heart.

3　Now let your mind wander over the idea of a temple. What elements are important for you to include? Should it be a physical building or somewhere out in nature? What are its boundaries like? A temple needs to be defined. If it is located outdoors, think in terms of a ring of trees, perhaps; or a circle of stones. Perhaps it could be on a small island, or surrounded by a beautiful old wall?

4   Feel the materials used to create your temple. What is the floor like? Is it marble and cool underfoot, or warm polished wood? Do your toes curl on woodland moss or feel sun-kissed sand? What are the walls made of? Are there windows? What is the temperature in your space?

5   What decoration does your temple have? Are there tapestries, stained-glass windows, sacred symbols, or is it plain?

6   Imagine the altar. Is it carved from wood or made of rough-hewn stone? What items will you have on it? Traditionally, one would have something to represent each element—a candle for fire, incense for air, salt or bread for earth, and water or wine for water. How does the incense smell? Feel the salt run through your fingers; break off a piece of the bread. Lift the cup (what kind of cup?) to your nose and smell the wine or sweet freshness of the water.

7   What would you wear in your temple? Feel the fabric (if indeed you are wearing clothes) against your body. Look at your feet.

8   Every temple has a guardian, whether it be an angel, a nature spirit, or a power animal. What would be the guardian of your temple? Do you already have a connection with it? If not, could you make one?

If you find this exercise difficult, let me give you a blueprint for a temple which works very effectively for me.

THE TEMPLE OF MALKUTH

This temple already has a lot of power and comfort invested in it as it is one of the temples on the Tree of Life. Malkuth is the "earth" temple. It is based on one described by Dolores Ashcroft-Nowicki.

The temple is square with black and white tiles on the floor. An altar sits in the middle, made of two handcrafted cubes of black wood (one on top of the other), well polished by loving hands.

Over the altar lies a linen cloth and on top of that is a bowl made of electric-blue crystal. Inside the bowl, a light burns steadily. Next to it sits a loaf of freshly baked bread and a bronze cup containing a rich, fruity red wine.

Above the altar, hanging down from the ceiling, is a bronze censor burning sandalwood incense.

In one wall are three heavy oak doors, with no handles or locks. In front of the doors are two pillars, which stretch from floor to ceiling. The pillar on the left (as you look at them), is made of gleaming black ebony. The pillar on the right shines a soft silver.

The other three walls all have rich colored, stained-glass windows. On the window behind you, there is an eagle, soaring into the sky. In the right-hand window is a winged lion, surrounded by flames. In the left-hand window is a winged bull, stamping on the earth. Note how similar these are to the Native American power animals. If you wish, you could substitute bear for lion and buffalo for bull.

The guardian of the Temple of Malkuth is the archangel Sandalphon. Imagine him as a tall young man with eyes full of wisdom and compassion, tinged with sadness (he feels keenly how we hurt our Mother Earth). He wears a long robe, which shimmers with the hues of autumn: russet red, gold, earthy brown, and soft green.

1   Spend time in this temple. Look around you and ponder the meaning of the symbols. Meditate on them and see if you find any illumination.

2   Talk to Sandalphon—with deep respect. Ask for his teachings. Listen in silence.

3   Clean the temple. Imagine making it sparkle—get down on your knees and scrub! Replace the bread and wine every day. Yes, it's metaphorical spring-cleaning but no less real for that.

4   Spend time sitting in front of the altar and meditate by gazing at the living flame.

5   Remember that this is a supremely safe place. If you ever feel anxious or worried, you can always come here to retreat. Ask Sandalphon for help in transforming your negative feelings. As you leave, imagine any negative energy being purified by the flame on the altar.

JOURNEYING

---- ✦ ----

Once you have built your temple, you can use it as the base for a series of explorations into the energetic worlds which surround us. Many mystical and magical traditions use a technique involving creative visualization to move in worlds other than our material everyday world. There are several ways of doing this:

FREEFORM JOURNEYING

This is very much a case of "let's go and see what happens." It's often used in shamanic traditions where there are believed to be three energy worlds: this world, the lower realm, and the upper realm. You start off in your temple and either descend or ascend. A door might open, with steps leading down (to the lower realm) or up (to the upper realm). Many people use a visualization of a hollow tree—going down through its roots to the lower realm and climbing up to the top, to the upper world (like Jack, of Jack and the Beanstalk—on his classic "journey").

Take a symbolic guardian with you (maybe an angel, a spirit animal, or guide) because you may come across some strange, and possibly even frightening, people or creatures. Remember these are "your" creatures and probably need dealing with. So—ask them what their purpose is and what you need to do. Your guardian can act as a protector and psychic bodyguard, so the experience is not too scary.

When you come back from your journeying, make sure you ground yourself well. Stomp your feet, have a drink and something to eat. Write down your experiences and insights.

GUIDED JOURNEYING

I actually think it helps (particularly for beginners) to have some kind of blueprint for your journey. The most effective tools for this kind of journeying are the tarot cards or the runes. In the Kabbalistic tradition, you would gradually ascend the Tree of Life, experiencing each sephirah and the pathway between them (each of which is governed by a tarot card).

If you don't want to work up the tree systematically, you can use any card or rune as a doorway to energy-journeying. I find tarot cards easier to use and prefer the classic Rider Waite pack as the cards feature such clear, figurative images; but choose a pack that resonates with you.

1   Pick out a card. You may know the card with which you wish to work—or you may decide to allow fate to take a hand and just pluck one from the pack.

2   Sit or lie quietly. Focus on your breathing and center yourself by breathing into your solar plexus chakra.

3   Now, construct your inner temple. Imagine every detail and walk into it, feeling your feet on its floor.

4   Imagine a curtain before you. In the Malkuth temple it would hang over the middle door; it could, however, hang from two trees or rocks—or just appear in thin air. (Energetic worlds do not need to follow the same rules as the physical one.)

5   As you gaze at the curtain, an image of your tarot card appears on it, as if on a tapestry. See the card in all its detail.

6   As you walk closer to the curtain, you notice that the image is alive and moving. The edges seem to blur and blend into the world outside.

7   Walk into the curtain and feel yourself step from one world to another—into the world of the tarot card. Look at the scene around you. What happens next? Some cards invite you to walk further into their landscape. Some seem to demand that you meet and converse with the beings depicted. Follow your instinct.

8   Hopefully, you will gain some important insights or learn some new knowledge. When you feel you are ready, turn around and walk back. The curtain will appear again and you should walk through it (remembering to thank any beings with whom you have spoken for their advice or insights).

9   As you walk back into your temple, the curtain will fade away. Spend some time thinking about your experience. You may want to discuss it with Sandalphon or your guardian. Give thanks at the altar before you go.

BRINGING SPIRITUAL ENERGY INTO YOUR CELLS

---- ✴ ----

This exercise pulls vital energy into your body to be used in whatever way you need. You can focus purely on its spiritual quality, or direct it for physical or emotional healing. For ease, I'm using the chakra system here.

1 Send your attention up to the crown chakra. Imagine it revolving vigorously, absorbing spiritual energy from the higher planes and transforming it so you can use it on the lower plane.

2 Visualize (and feel) this energy flowing like a silver stream down and through the left-hand side of your head, neck, body, and the leg. Exhale slowly as it descends.

3 As you slowly inhale, visualize the current passing from the sole of the left foot to the sole of the right foot and gradually ascending the right-hand side of the body. From the head, it returns to the crown. Continue this circulation for several breaths until the flow is firmly established.

4 Visualize the flow of spiritual energy streaming from the crown down the front of the face, chest, and down to the feet where it turns under the soles of the feet and goes up the back to the crown again. Exhale as it goes down the front; inhale as it comes up the back. Continue for several breaths until the flow is firmly established.

5 Focus your attention on the base chakra. Imagine this power and energy being drawn up through the body through all the other chakras (the central sephiroth), to the crown. It shoots up the body, and erupts through the crown like a fountain of light and energy. The fountain showers down around your body, outlining the aura. Inhale as the energy ascends the body; exhale as it showers down.

6 Imagine your body surrounded by bright spiritual energy. Every cell is being suffused by this divine energy. This is the time to direct the energy, if you wish.

HONORING DARK ENERGY

CHAPTER TWELVE

Strive for the light, always the light. We are living in a society obsessed with the bright, the light, and the positive. Within this gleaming world, there is no room for shadow, for penumbra, twilight, or darkness. We have turned our backs on the harsher, more difficult side of life—we just don't want to know about it.

New Age consciousness has promoted a world of permanent sunshine, of bright colors, rainbows, smiles, and hugs. Its buzzwords are love, light, joy, peace, and beauty. Its key concepts are affirmations, angels, and positive thought. We are taught that we can "never afford the luxury of a negative thought", let alone negative emotions or actions. The message is that our lives should be permanently sunny, happy, and joyous; all of our relationships must be loving; all our spirits coursing towards the light. We are expected to be superhumans, always up, always cheerful, and always bright.

Is this natural? Is it realistic? Of course not. We all have times when we feel down, depressed, or negative; times when we feel consumed with less than ideal emotions such as anger, hate, jealousy, or self-pity. Should we expunge such emotions immediately, drowning them in positive affirmations and self-talk? Or do we do ourselves a disfavor by ignoring the dark and always seeking the light? Do we miss the subtlety of the moon's shadows by always craving the clear illumination of the sun?

Life is made up of darkness as well as light. We cannot put a veneer on "negative" emotions and hope they will simply go away. In fact, the more we disown these emotions, the more harm they will do. It's like finding a patch of nasty damp in your house. You could face it square on and root out the cause, or you could simply paper over it and try to forget about it. If you go the latter route, it looks fine for a while but eventually the damp breaks out again, far worse than before.

We only have to look at nature to see that there are times of growth, and times of decay. Sometimes, day, light, and the upward surge of life hold

sway; sometimes we are in the grip of night and dark, and the death-hush lies over the earth. We are ignoring an essential truth if we seek to live always in the light. After all, in order to have a peak (a mountain), you must have a trough (a valley). How can we truly know happiness if we have never experienced sadness and gloom?

By denying the dark, we also lose the chance for genuine self-understanding and growth. There are many lessons and much wisdom to learn amid the shadows. We can and should sacrifice the idea of perfection. We all contain within us both good and evil, light and shade. When we turn and face our darkness, our demons of the night, we may find revelations beyond our wildest dreams—for there is dark energy too.

The ancients knew this and knew it well. In the Kabbalah, the Tree of Life has a shadow image, a dark reflection. On it, are all the sins and temptations known: the archdemons of the soul. In many cultures, the gods and goddesses are not just pure and good but complex creations; they have as many differing moods and attributes as we humans. Many ancient initiation ceremonies demanded that the initiate descend into the bowels of the earth, or deep into the forest, or out onto the untamed sea to face his or her demons; to conquer fear, embrace the dark and return transformed, into the light.

I am not saying that affirmations and positive thoughts are bad things. They can be incredibly useful and worthwhile, particularly if you are the kind of person who constantly dwells on the negative. They are also valuable lessons in the first stages of energy-working. But once you have reached a certain level of skill in this work, you no longer need to put a gloss on life. You need to face the dark energy, to plumb the depths: only then can you truly scale the heights. Our first task is to face the shadow.

SEEKING
OUR SHADOW

✳

When I was small, I used to peer under the bed, petrified of the dark beast that I was convinced laid underneath. I had nightmares of a black, cat-like creature, which stalked me throughout my childhood, my teens, and into adulthood. For years, I sought to avoid and ignore it, hoping it would forget me and go away. It wasn't until I started to study Jungian psychology and became fascinated with art therapy that I dared face "my beast". My black beast turned out to be something quite wonderful: she was my own repressed animal self, my wild feminine energy, my sensuality, and my inner "wild woman". She appeared as I painted: first as a terrifying monster that I barely dared look at, and gradually transforming into a powerful Sekhmet, the Egyptian lion goddess. Next, she became a sinuous dancer and then a delicious strumpet. I realized that here was a huge part of myself, which I had denied and repressed. She contained my shadow material, my dark energy, which craved release.

In Jungian psychology, the shadow carries everything that we push aside during our waking, conscious life: all the qualities that do not fit with our ideal image of ourselves, and everything which makes us embarrassed, shameful, and small. The shadow can be full of hate, rage, jealousy, shame, laziness, aggression, greed, lust, or untrammeled sexuality. The shadow comes to us most strongly in our dreams, as that frightening "other"— usually the same sex as ourselves. She or he is the vicious murderer, the cunning thief, the loudmouthed zealot, the overbearing teacher, the pathetic wimp, the down-and-out, and the whining child. Our shadow often surfaces when we "lose it". Something triggers us and we hit out in a sudden uncharacteristic bout of fury, or we get blind drunk and wake up next to a stranger, feeling stunned and horrified that we just "weren't ourselves" last night. We weren't ourselves—we were our shadow.

The shadow isn't always negative, it can also be full of wild wonderful energy. If we have ever been told we are "too much", "too loud", "too sexy", we have suppressed wonderful things as well. The aim here isn't to destroy the shadow but to integrate it into our conscious lives, so its immense hidden energy can be used for our own good.

SHADOW-WORKING

Try these ways to unleash and integrate shadow material:

✴ Who really annoys you? It could be someone close, someone you don't know, even someone on television. Which qualities are particularly irritating?

✴ Now think of any groups of people you really can't stand; that you find frightening or repulsive or unpleasant. Be brutally honest—even if your thoughts seem atrocious.

✴ We project our shadows onto other people so the chances are that the qualities you hate in someone else will be what is hidden in your own shadow. Think about it. Is the hated quality something you possess in yourself, or that lies hidden within you?

✴ Keep a dream journal and notice the shadow figures. It will always be the one who enacts the dark and forbidden: the thief, the murderer, the rapist, the sadist, or the beast. When you have found some of shadow characters, you can start working with them.

THE "OTHER CHAIR" TECHNIQUE

Sit on one chair and imagine your shadow character on the other. Start a dialogue. Ask them why they behave the way they do. What do they dislike about you? What do they want to say? What do you want to say to them? Record your "conversation" so you can replay it later—you may find surprises.

PAINT YOUR SHADOW

This can be very powerful. I found it therapeutic to paint large on a huge sheet of paper on the wall. Maybe paint in candlelight or the dark (the shadow seems to emerge more readily then than in daylight). You can close your eyes, or paint with your nondominant hand. Just paint freely. Once you have finished, try talking to your painting. Take the image and use the "other chair" technique to see your shadow's point of view, or write it a letter.

WRITE TO YOUR SHADOW FIGURE

Free associate and see what emerges. It could be a dialogue; it could be a narrative; it could be a poem or a play. Maybe the shadow figure itself wants to write. What would it say? How would it express itself?

Be on the watch for shadow material. Watch out for irritating people and analyze why they grate on you. Whom do you envy? What would you love to be able to say, but feel you can't? What are your deepest desires; your most wild fantasies? What are you hiding when you overeat, drink to excess, take drugs, overwork, or binge on box sets? What parts of your life are you denying?

These are the thoughts we dare not think, maybe because we fear that we would have to play out our fantasies. That is not the case. Often, all our psyche needs is to air the possibilities, to find small, safe ways to unleash our shadow self. Your inner wild woman or man might cherish a swim in the sea, or half an hour staring up at the clouds. Our inner fighter might need to unleash some energy by boxing, or screaming out loud where no one can hear. Simple things might fit the bill. If you're not sure, ask your shadow.

PLUMBING THE DEPTHS

Sometimes life overwhelms us; we are consumed by grief or depression, anxiety or fear. Most of our lives are spent desperately running away from who we are. We avoid ourselves in myriad ways—through overwork, alcohol, drugs, being busy, watching television, going out, or being with other people. We are scared of standing alone, quiet, and naked before the vastness of the universe. We are terrified of looking at ourselves honestly and facing what gazes back at us. Those who sink into darkness and gloom are perhaps just a little more honest—they peer through the curtains of illusion. They see the depths but just cannot reach out.

We also cling, desperately, to our "story"—what happened to us; our situation; our roles. Often we blame other people, situations, or events that happened years ago for our present misery. Yes, terrible things that have happened in the past can affect us in the present. Past trauma needs to be teased out, gently and compassionately. Yet, many of us stay in thrall to the past and become its permanent victim. We relinquish our own power, and our own energy by doing so.

One way to pull back our power is to face our own dark energy. When we make a descent into the underworld, we face the worst that could possibly happen—the stripping of everything we hold dear. Then, when we stand alone, without our worldly trappings, without our stories, we realize just who we are—how we have an essential self who transcends all the glitter and ego. It's an empowering experience.

Many people who suffer grief follow a descent, naturally. Sometimes the psyche just needs to shut down, to rest. Others descend at a transition phase of their lives, often at midlife when priorities start to shift. Such descents can be deeply painful and support from a skilled counselor or psychotherapist can help. However, a controlled mini-descent is a process we can do at any time (and may prevent a full-on descent). It is a process that can challenge many of our assumptions about ourselves. It is a meeting with dark energy that can, paradoxically, bring more bright light vital energy into your life than you could imagine.

THE DESCENT OF INNANA

For this descent, I borrow from the myth of Inanna. Inanna was a Sumerian queen and goddess from around the 3rd millennium BCE. Sumer was located in what is now Iraq. Back then, it was green and fertile, a true Garden of Eden. Inanna was a complex goddess, yet she also led a normal life as ruler, wife, lover, and mother. Then she descended to the underworld, to meet her sister (and shadow) Ereshkigal. On the way she is stripped of everything, until she stands before Ereshkigal naked.

You may want to record this visualization, or ask someone to read it to you.

1   Find a place that is safe, dark, comfortable, and warm. Lie down and spend a few minutes focusing on your breathing.

2   Visualize yourself as Inanna, the great Queen of Sumer. You sit on a throne, enjoying power and prestige. You are rich and powerful. You have a partner, friends, children maybe, a home, a career. You want for nothing. Yet something is missing. You feel a need to visit your dark sister Ereshkigal who lives in the gloom of the underworld. You kiss your family goodbye and, dressed in your best clothes and finest jewelery, you set off on your journey.

3   You walk through fields of swaying corn, dotted with poppies and cornflowers. Birds are singing and the sun shines brightly. The whole world seems beautiful and part of you yearns to sit and picnic before returning home. You see ahead of you a range of mountains, and you know that your quest leads you there.

4   You come to a fast-flowing stream with stepping stones, leading to a dark cave. As you walk into the shadow of the rocks, you feel a chill run over your body. You step into the cave and suddenly all the light and warmth of the world has vanished.

5   You pick up a tiny lantern.
At the back of the cave lies,
a small passageway. You
squeeze yourself through
it and go along a narrow
corridor. The path leads
steeply downward and you
feel as if you are journeying
into the bowels of the earth.

6   Suddenly, a large figure
looms before you. It is Neti,
the Chief Gatekeeper of
the Underworld. Behind
him lies the first gate that
leads to Ereshkigal's realm.
"Welcome," says Neti, "if
you would come to the Dark
Kingdom you must shed your
fine crown." You take off the
crown and with it all your lofty
aspirations, your pretentions
to spirituality, your feeling
of being better than other
people. You drop that "holier
than thou" aspect and walk
through the gate with Neti.

7   On you walk, down and down,
until you reach another gate.
Neti asks you if you want to
continue and, when you say
yes, he asks for your earrings.

With these you have to give up
the pride you feel over your
special abilities, your sense
of being different. You take
off the earrings and become
quite ordinary.

8   Down, down the path goes—
and before you is another
gate. This time Neti asks for
your necklace and you give
it up, along with your power
of speech, your clever words,
your witty repartee, and your
bright conversation. You leave
behind your intellect, your
quick mind, and your smart
thoughts. Neti allows you to
go on, further into the dark
and deep.

9   The next gate looms and
here you are asked to give
up the beautiful breastplate,
which covers your heart. Here
you leave behind all affairs
of the heart, relationships,
emotional attachments, your
roles as partner, lover, child,
and friend. Feeling quite cold
and alone, you walk through
the gate.

10 At the next gate, Neti asks for the thick belt that winds around your solar plexus. He takes with it your power and will, your intentions and desires. All your striving and strategies fall away.

11 You are now getting deep into the bowels of the earth and the sixth gate comes into view through the darkness. Neti smiles grimly, and you hand him the shimmering skirt which kept your lower body covered. With it, he takes your sexuality and sensuality, your reproductive powers, your role as parent or potential parent.

12 Now it is getting very cold. You shiver as you reach the seventh and final gate. You hand over your sandals. With them, Neti takes your home, your place on the earth, your center, and your security. You are left naked and vulnerable.

13 You come into the presence of your sister, Ereshkigal, the Dark Goddess of the Underworld. She is huge and frightening and you feel very small. Take a while to recognize the feelings that come up. How does it feel to stand naked, with nothing? What do you recognize in Ereshkigal? What does she make you face? Can you see that you two are parts of one whole?

14 You step forward and Ereshkigal strikes you dead with a glance. She picks up your body and hangs it on a meat hook. You recognize that the physical you is being swept away, yet the essential "you" still remains. What is this "you"? Who are you without your story? How does it feel to have nothing left of ordinary reality?

15 Slowly, you become aware that you have the chance to return to life. How would you like to return? What qualities will you take with you? What will you leave behind? This is a powerful chance to shed anything that you no longer want or need; to abandon old forms of behavior that no longer serve you.

16 Ereshkigal gently lifts you down and holds you to her breast. You feel her now as warm and sisterly, not an avenging death goddess. She breathes life into you, and you feel fresh, like a newborn baby. You thank her for the lessons you have learned, and you hug, as equals. You promise you will integrate her dark energy into your life. She hands you a simple white linen dress and a pair of sandals.

17 Slowly, you retrace your steps through the seven gates (steps 13 back to 6). At each one, Neti offers you your own adornments. Do you want them? Do you want to re-evaluate them? Think carefully before you take them back or discard them totally. You may wish to come back later, or to postpone your decision.

18 Eventually, you come back out into the sunlight and step across the stream once more. The world seems very beautiful in the soft late afternoon sun. You feel the earth beneath your feet and give thanks for the gifts of life. You remember the people you love, and give thanks for good relationships. You ponder what is good and fine in your life and determine that you won't take it for granted again. You ponder on those elements of your life that aren't serving you and decide which you will let go or change. Now you have been on the meat hook, there are no trials you cannot face. You have been to the underworld, met your shadow, and given up the delusions of life. Now you can be reborn.

DEATH—
THE END OF ENERGY?

CHAPTER THIRTEEN

Death. The final taboo. We live our lives trying to ignore it, push it away, and pretend it won't happen—at least not to us. Yet the unpalatable and inescapable truth is that we all die. So why are we so frightened of death? Slowly, we are seeing a shift towards talking about and pondering death. We're seeing the rise of death doulas, of coffin clubs; we're becoming more open to discussion of our mortality. Yet even so, what often emerges is fear.

Maybe our fear comes about because we think of ourselves in terms of our egos, our personality. We spend our lives bolstering our egos, surrounding ourselves with symbols of security and status—we build a comfort cocoon to shield ourselves and block out anything unpleasant. We keep ourselves busy—frenetically busy—whether that involves working like crazy or vegging out with Netflix. We avoid thinking about life, let alone death. We are scared of losing our friends, our families, our pets, our homes, and our standing in life. The fear comes about because we have not grasped the most important fact about energy. As energy beings we are not separate from life or death—we are not ego-bound individuals struggling on our own; we are part of the whole.

People who have had near-death experiences talk of seeing lights, hearing sounds, feeling themselves uplifted and filled with transcendent energy, and of being pulled towards a source of power and light and energy. These are concepts that energy-workers understand. Ancient traditions refer to the various energy bodies that are released in death, allowing the soul finally to escape its material shackles and become pure energy once more. When we die, we ascend the Tree of Life, becoming purer and purer energy as we leave behind our material shell.

DEATHWORKING

✳

The paradoxical point about death is that it can make life so much richer.
You hear about people who find out that they only have months, or weeks,
to live. Instead of sinking into depression, they make the most of their
time. Many discover wonderful truths about themselves: they uncover
huge reserves of strength, power, and character. Some find amazing
routes to healing and don't die then at all. The thought of dying focuses
the spirit like nothing else. Of course, you don't have to wait—you could
start living right now…

A YEAR TO LIVE

What would you do if you had only a month to live? A week to live? A day
to live? An hour to live? Why not live every day as if it were your last? Don't
imagine you have limitless time. Don't let fear or shame hold you back.

The following exercise is incredibly powerful. If you have followed the
Inanna descent from the previous chapter, you should find you have
already done the groundwork. Even if you find it distasteful, do try to put
aside some time to consider the following.

1   Imagine you only had one year left to live. How would you
    spend that year?

2   Would you give up your work or change your job?

3   Who would you see more of; who would you see less of?

4   Write letters to all the people you love and cherish. Tell
    them how important they have been to you. Tell them
    what you appreciate about them. Maybe you should send
    these letters now, before it's too late.

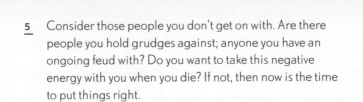

5 Consider those people you don't get on with. Are there people you hold grudges against; anyone you have an ongoing feud with? Do you want to take this negative energy with you when you die? If not, then now is the time to put things right.

6 Who could you help during your final year? Who could benefit from your time, your energy, your money? Why not try to help them now?

7 Review your life. Is there anything you regret not doing; or anything you always wanted to do? Why not think about doing it now?

8 Did you make mistakes? Could you put those right? If not, let them go, don't waste energy on them. If there's something that could be done, why put it off?

My favorite quote regarding death comes from Stephen Levine, author of *Who Dies?* and *A Year to Live* (both of which I highly recommend). Levine says:

"Of course, the reason that some part of us denies that it will die is because it never does… the reason something within feels immortal is because it is."

In some philosophies, the concept of death simply doesn't exist. We just move from one state of being into another; from one kind of energy to a different kind. As we have seen throughout this book, the universe is pure consciousness, pure energy—once we die we simply remove many of the veils preventing us from seeing the true nature of being.

WHERE WERE YOU BEFORE YOU WERE BORN?

Ponder this question: who were you before you were born? Where were you? Look into a small baby's eyes and there is usually something strange and knowing in them. If only they could tell us what they have seen and where they have come from. We've all been through birth: we survived. We came from somewhere into this body, this life—and we will depart back to that place. The mystery is that we cannot remember.

Try this exercise:

1   Make yourself comfortable in a warm, safe place. Lie down and bring your attention to the breath, focusing on the solar plexus.

2   Slowly, go back through your life. Review where you are now—what you are doing, who you are with, how you feel. Then slowly, scroll back through your life without dwelling or judgment.

3   Take yourself back to your teenage years. Then to your childhood. What do you remember? What was important? Can you recall your first day at school? Where was your first home? How far back can you reach?

4   When you can't remember any more, start to imagine. See yourself as a toddler, as a baby. If you have seen photographs, put yourself into them.

5   You are lying in your cot. Now go back further still. You are being born. You are being pushed down through the birth canal, squeezed and pressed into life. You emerge into the world and open your mouth to breathe—and cry. Stay with this for a while—how does it feel?

<u>6</u>   Now, imagine you are in the womb: warm, enclosed, surrounded by the gentle waters of the amniotic fluid. You hear your mother's heartbeat above you, the gurgling of her stomach. You can easily go back further still, to a time when you were not even in physical form.

<u>7</u>   You are in the other place. How does it feel? How do you feel? Spend some time just being in this pure energy form. Feel the freedom.

<u>8</u>   Remember why you decided to come to earth, to take a physical form. From a distance you see your parents-to-be. What made you choose them? What lessons did you all need to learn? Your parentage was no accident—it was a conscious decision.

<u>9</u>   When you feel you have learned all you can, slowly bring your awareness back to your breath. Become aware of the room around you. Gently open your eyes. Stamp your feet to ground you. You may want to have a warm drink. Record your experiences in your journal.

The realization that you decided to be born, that you chose your parents and your situation in life, can be very liberating. At some level we decided to go through these experiences. We wanted to learn. What lessons are you here to learn? Will you ensure they are learned before you die or will you miss the opportunity?

THE
DARK PATH

※

Many spiritual teachings advise that we "practice" dying, that we walk the path we will take when we die. Then, when the soul is confronted with death, it automatically follows the process. This pathworking uses Greek mythology and is a natural progression from the Inanna descent we made in the last chapter. I also take this journey when anyone I know dies. By doing so, you can take the opportunity to talk with them, to conclude any unfinished business. You could help them make the transition to their new life. Some people become stuck in fear and trepidation. It is a great service to perform this ritual when there has been a disaster in which a lot of people died suddenly. Many souls feel lost and become "stuck" in the shadows. You can help them. Let's take a visit to the underworld:

1   We start in the Temple of Malkuth. Spend some time building the temple as on page 156. Greet Sandalphon and approach the altar. On it, you notice there is a wide bronze bowl that contains a pile of silver coins. Take a handful and put them in the deep pocket of your robe.

2   Between the pillars, you see the tarot card of The World. As you watch the curtain it becomes three-dimensional; the colors swirl and you walk forwards into it and through it. You are in a field of swaying corn, dotted with poppies and cornflowers. Birds are singing and the sun shines brightly. You see ahead of you the familiar range of mountains and walk toward them.

3   You come to the stream and walk over the stepping stones to the dark cave.

4   A voice speaks out from the gloom; it is Hecate, the Wise Woman. She asks why you have come and you tell her that you wish to descend to the kingdom of Persephone and Hades. She points to a small opening at the back of the cave and gives you a lamp to guide you.

5   You squeeze through the opening and find yourself in a small tunnel, which runs

steeply downward. The walls close in around you and, as you follow the path, you can feel the rock pressing in, squeezing you, as if you were being born. Sometimes you have to crawl, sometimes squeeze through narrow stretches. Eventually, the path opens out and you find yourself in a vast cavern, lit by flickering torches.

6 Beneath your feet is fine sand. You are standing on the shore of a great river. Charon, ferryman of the dead, stands by his boat. Around him throng the souls of the dead; those who cannot make the crossing. Is there anyone here you know? If so, talk to them, resolve any unfinished business. Say your farewells and give them one of your silver coins so they can cross the river.

7 If there isn't anyone you know, pass out your coins to the others. Bless them and send them on their way back to the source of all energy. Keep back two coins for yourself. Hand one to Charon and get into his boat. Slowly, he rows across the river and you get out the other side.

8 Before you are gates, which swing open as you approach. Hades and Persephone sit on thrones in a great hall. You walk forward and stand before them, looking into their eyes. Surprisingly, they are not stern or terrifying but kind and laughing. You realize they are not just the King and Queen of the Dead but the Lord and Lady of Rebirth.

9 Hades leads you to a mirror and asks you to look into it. You see your true self, as it was before you took bodily form and as it will be after you relinquish your body. What do you see? What is your true essence? You realize that beyond our looks, our personality, our hopes, and fears, our possessions, lies the real us—a timeless, deathless, energetic essence.

10 Persephone steps forward and embraces you. Your body seems to disappear as you float up to the stars with her. You become the stars also. You shimmer with energy and a pure sense of bliss.

11 Gently, Persephone breathes on your face and tells you that it is not yet time for you

to become a being of pure energy, rejoining the source of all love and light. Softly, she carries you down again to the great hall.

12 Smiling, you leave and retrace your steps. Charon accepts your other silver coin and rows you back across the lake. You promise the souls waiting that you will return with more coins for them. This time, you find your way back to the cave easily. Hecate takes the lamp and smiles gently. You look into her eyes and can no longer tell if she is a very old woman or a young girl.

13 As you walk out of the cave your eyes blink to adjust to the light. The world seems beautiful and you resolve to make the most of your life. The tarot card of The World hangs between two trees and you step through it and back to the Temple of Malkuth.

14 Sandalphon greets you and you spend a few moments sharing your experience with him and giving thanks. He reminds you that you should walk this path often—for yourself and for the lost souls who have forgotten their connection to the source.

CLAIMING OUR
ENERGETIC HERITAGE

Most of us curtail our energy with our fears and suspicions: we only half live. Releasing the fear of death and discovering our true nature provides huge liberation.

The path we have followed in this book has been a curious one. I hope you have found it as beneficial and eye-opening as I have. By now, you have probably realized that *The Energy Secret* isn't really a "secret" at all—it is something for all of us to share. In the years to come, I am quite sure that working with energy will seem the most natural thing in the world. In fact, it will seem strange not to use this wonderful power, this essence, to its full capacity. For without knowledge and use of our own energy, we just don't live to our full potential.

Incorporating energy into your everyday life makes each day an adventure, a learning process, and a step further along our lifelong path. It starts simply by helping us to get back in touch with our bodies and discover better health. It progresses by informing our relationships—with our selves, with each other, with friends, family, work colleagues, and even complete strangers. It ends by linking us with our spirituality and our eternal nature, as beings of pure energy and light. The pathway is one of great joy but also sadness. Sometimes it is an easy path to take, and sometimes difficult and painful. Yet as we begin to feel energy moving in our bodies and in our lives, we start to discover the true secret. We begin to know ourselves for what we truly are—we understand the nature of our being and our true heritage. We learn to live with energy, to work with energy, to be energy.

I hope you enjoy the journey and look forward to meeting you—as we all will meet—at the source of all energy and light.

INDEX

A
air 122, 124–5
air purifiers 119, 144
allies 96–7, 117
animals 121, 132
  animal sexuality 110
  auras 28
  in dreams 88
  power animals 96–7, 117, 158, 160
aromatherapy 119–20, 124, 144
asanas 74
Ashcroft-Nowicki, Dolores 158
attention, paying attention exercise 18
auras 27–30, 164
  how to start seeing 28–9, 141
  seeing someone else's 28, 141
  seeing your own 30
Ayurveda 40, 60, 62

B
Bach, Dr Edward 52
Bach Flower Essences 52–4, 124
back bends 106
base chakra 33
  bringing spiritual energy into your cells 164
  contacting through sound 38, 118
  energetic connections 147
  sensing the energy of your home 115
Baubo 110
The Bible 55
Binah 154
Biodanza 35, 78, 79–80, 90
birds 132, 141, 142
blues, banishing 45
the body
  body energy 12–81
  feeling energy within 14–16
  getting in touch with 17–20
  healing therapies for 40–59
bonding exercises, creating energetic rapport 98–9
bone-balancing exercise 19

breathing exercises 20, 22–6, 27
  the breath of fire 25
  color breathing 58
  the complete breath 23
  connecting with the breath 104
  healing chakras 35
  liberating emotional energy 90
  therapeutic breathwork 26
Breathpod 26
brow chakra 36–7
  contacting through sound 39
  energetic connections 147
  shielding techniques 94
Buddha 27, 96, 144
Buddhism 22
Butler, W E 150

C
candles 123, 144
chakras 30–9, 87
  balancing for health and harmony 30–9
  bringing spiritual energy into your cells 164
  channeling healing energy 48, 49
  color and 122
  contacting through sound 38–9, 55, 118
  dealing with other people's energy 93
  energy baths 141
  getting in touch with 31, 125
  kissing 109
  looking at the 33–7
  making energetic connections 147
  sensing the energy of your home 115
  shielding techniques 94
  Tree of Life and 152
  see also individual chakras
Charon 184, 185
Chesed 154
Chockmah 155
Christ 27
Christianity 62

cities 138–42
  city energy 139–42
  city medicine 141–2
  conscious manifestation 142
  energy commuting 141
  space dancing 139
clapping 117
cleansing 116–18
clearing techniques 117–18
clutter 116, 144
color 57–9
  bringing color into your home 122, 123
  color breathing 58
  color correspondences 59
  Tree of Life 152, 153, 154, 155
commuting, energy 141
conscious manifestation 142
cookery, spiritual 65
crafts, handmade 121
crown chakra 33, 36–7
  bringing spiritual energy into your cells 164
  channeling healing energy 48
  contacting through sound 39, 118
  creating energetic rapport 99
  dealing with other people's energy 93
  energy baths 141
  sensing the energy of your home 115
  shielding techniques 94
crystals 123, 125, 144

D
Daath 154
dan tien 78
dance
  Biodanza 35, 78, 79–80
  energy of the dance 78–81
  liberating emotional energy 90
dark energy
  descent of Innana 173–6
  honoring 166–76
  plumbing the depths 172
  seeking our shadows 169–76

death 178–85
  the dark path 183–5
  deathworking 179–82
decluttering 116, 144
depression 60, 172
despondency or despair 54
DNA, epigenetics 84–5
Dossey, Larry 63
dragon stamping 73
dreams
  liberating emotional energy 91
  recording your 88–9, 91, 170

E
earth energy 125
  listening to 129
  reconnecting with 127–9
emotional energy 82–111
  creating energetic rapport 98–9
  dealing with other people's 92–5
  guardians and allies 96–7
  liberating 90–1
  sexual energy 100–11
  shielding techniques 94–5
  tracking unwanted 86–9
  working with 84–99
energy
  body energy 12–81
  concept of 8–11
  emotional energy 82–111
  energy exercise 68–81
  energy games 50
  environmental energy 112–47
  sexual energy 100–11
  spiritual energy 148–85
energy bubbles 94–5, 96, 99, 147
environmental energy 112–47
  balancing elemental energy with your home 122–5
  bringing color into your home 122
  cities and the workplace 138–47
  decluttering and cleansing 116–18
  feng shui and vastu shastra 119–21
  natural energy 126–37

epigenetics 84–5
Ereshkigal 110, 173–6
Estes, Clarissa Pinkola 110
exercise, energy 68–81
eye strain 41

F
fans 124
fear 53
feng shui 114, 119–21, 122, 144
fire 122, 123
fish 121
Five Rhythms 35, 78
flower essences 52–4, 124
flowers 121, 144
food
  creating with loving energy 64
  energetic power of 60–7
  making mealtimes special 67
  soul shopping and spiritual cookery 65
  spirit and soul food 62–4

G
Geburah 153–4
genes, epigenetics 84–5
gods and goddesses 110, 168
Goldman, Jonathan 39, 55
Grad, Bernard 63
Greek mythology 183
grief 172
Grof, Stanislav and Christina 26
Guardian Angel 153
guardians 96–7, 117, 160
the gut 60

H
Hades 183, 184
hands, awakening your 46
headaches 41, 42
healing therapies for the body 40–59
  channeling healing energy 48
  color therapy 57–9
  energy games 50
  flower essences 52–4
  healing 46–51

shiatsu 41–6
sound therapy 55
health, balancing chakras for 30–9
heart chakra 34–5
  channeling healing energy 48
  contacting through sound 38
  creating energetic rapport 99
  dealing with other people's energy 93
  energetic connections 147
  energy baths 141
heart searching exercise 19
Hecate 183, 185
Himmelsbach, Helga 74
Hinduism 62
Hod 153
Holotropic BreathworkTM 26
homes
  balancing elemental energy with 122–5
  bringing color into 122
  decluttering and cleansing 116–18
  energy of the 114–25
  feng shui and vastu shastra 119–21
  the energy of your home 115
hypnotherapy 37

I
I Ching 146
Inanna, descent of 173–6
incense 118, 124
indigenous people 130
insomnia, soothing 45
Islam 62

J
journals 35
  deathworking 182
  dream 88–9, 91, 170
journeying 160–3
  freeform journeying 160
  guided journeying 162–3
Judaism 62, 151
Jungian psychology 169

K
Kabbalah 16, 55, 150, 151–5, 162, 168
Kether 154, 155
ki 40
kindness, random acts of 147
kissing 109
Kravitz, Dr Judith 26
Kundalini 78, 111
!Kung San 78

L
Laskow, Leonard 62–3
law of attraction 142
leaves, stone and leaf energy 127
Levine, Stephen 180
Linn, Denise 89
Lipton, Bruce 85
loving energy, creating food with 64
LSD (lysergic acid diethylamide) 26

M
Malkuth 152
  Temple of 158–9, 183, 185
mantras 55
marmas 40
massage, sensual 107
materials, natural 121
mealtimes, making them special 67
medicine path 132, 139
meditation
  exercise as 68
  healing chakras 37
  mealtimes 67
  Tree of Life and 151, 152
meetings, energetic 147
mindful walking 141
mirrors 123
Mohammed 27

N
Native Americans 62, 114, 117, 158
natural energy 126–37

reconnecting with earth energy 127–9
sacred energy 133–4
seasonal energy 136
Shamanic path 130–2
Neti 174–5, 176
Netzach 153
num 78

O
objects, in dreams 88
offices
  energetic meetings 147
  office energy 143
  office magic 146
  the office sanctuary 144
ojas 60, 62
Om 96, 121
oracular systems 146
organs, getting in touch with your 20
Orr, Leonard 26
"other chair" technique 171

P
painting
  liberating emotional energy 90
  painting your dreams 89
  painting your shadow 171
Pan 110
parasympathetic nervous system 23, 79
pathworking 152
pebble therapy 45
people, in dreams 88
Persephone 183, 184–5
Pilates 35, 37
plants 28, 121, 132, 141–2, 144
power animals 96–7, 117, 158
prana 40
pranayama 23
psychoneuroimmunology 16
public transport 141

Q
qi 40, 70, 121
qigong 70

breathing 22
dragon stamping 73
healing chakras 35
starting posture 70–1, 141
turning the head
  and twisting the tail 72
qoya 78
quwa 40

R
rapport
  connecting with the breath 104
  creating energetic rapport 98–9
Rebirthing Breathwork 26
reflection, liberating emotional energy 91
Reid, Daniel 61
Reiki 46
Roth, Gabrielle 35, 78
runes 146, 162
Rutherford, Leo 78

S
sacral chakra 34–5, 38
sacred energy 133–4
sacred sexuality 108–9
  bringing into everyday life 101
sage cleansing 117–18
salt 125
Sandalphon 158, 159, 183, 185
Sandeman, Stuart 26
sattvic food 60, 62
scent, power of 119–20
seasonal energy 136
Seattle, Chief 130
the seesaw 105
Sekhmet 110, 169
senses 127, 136
sensuality
  cultivating 102
  playing with sensual energy 104–6
  sensual massage 107
sephirahs 152–5, 162
sephiroth 152, 164
serotonin 60
sexual energy 100–11

animal sexuality 110
bringing sacred sexuality into everyday life 101
cultivating sensuality 102
elemental sex 111
playing with sensual energy 104-6
raising energy with Tantra 111
sacred sexuality 108-9
sensual massage 107
uncovering the wild within 110
shadow working 169, 170-1
Shakti 78, 100, 111
shamanic traditions 134, 160
Shamanic path 130-2
shiatsu 41-6
banishing the blues 45
banishing headaches 41, 42
soothing insomnia 45
shielding techniques 94-5
Shiva 100, 110, 111, 144
shopping 138
soul shopping 65
sites, sacred 133-4
skin, cultivating sensuality 102
sleep
recording your dreams 88-9, 91, 170
soothing insomnia 45
smudging 114, 117-18
solar plexus chakra 34-5
contacting through sound 38, 118
energetic connections 147
sensing the energy of your home 115
shielding techniques 94
the soul
soul shopping 65
spirit and soul food 62-4
sound
allowing sound into your home 120-1
contacting chakras through 38-9, 55, 118
sound cleansing 118
sound therapy 55

sounds of nature 127
space dancing 139
spaces, naming 119
Spider Goddess 130
spider plants 121, 144
spirit and soul food 62-4
spirit animals 160
spirit guardians 96-7, 117
spiritual energy 144, 148-85
bringing it into your cells 164
building the inner temple 156-7
connecting to 150-65
death of energy 178-85
honoring dark energy 166-76
journeying 160-3
Kabbalah 150, 151-5
Temple of Malkuth 158-9
Tree of Life 151, 152-5
spring cleaning 116
starting posture 70-1, 141
stone and leaf energy 127
succulents 121, 144
Sufi 62
supermarkets 138
sympathetic nervous system 79

T
tai chi 70
Tantra 100, 109, 111
Tarot 146, 162
Tashidowa 74
temples
building the inner temple 156-7
journeying 160
Temple of Malkuth 158-9, 183, 185
throat chakra 36-7, 39, 118, 147
Tiphareth 153, 154
Toro, Rolando 79
Traditional Chinese Medicine (TCM) 61, 62
Transformational Breath® 26
trauma 84-5, 172
Tree of Life 151, 152-5, 162, 168
death 178
Temple of Malkuth 158-9
trees, auras 28

turning the head and twisting the tail 72

V
vastu shastra 114, 119-21
Vedic culture 55, 122
vegetables 65
Vishnu 27
visualizations
bringing spiritual energy into your cells 164
the dark path 183-5
descent of Innana 173-6
healing chakras 37
journeying 160-3
mealtimes 67
power animals 96-7
voicework, healing chakras 37

W
walking, exercise as meditation 68
water 119, 120-1, 144
watery homes 122, 124
Weston, Sue 139
White, Ian 52
wildness, uncovering the wild within 110
wind chimes 120
Wolf, Fred Alan 62
the workplace 138-47
energetic meetings 147
office energy 143
office magic 146
the office sanctuary 144
writing to your shadow figure 171

Y
Yesod 152
yoga 70, 74-7
back bends 106
the breath of fire 25
breathing 22-5
healing chakras 35
the seesaw 105
Tantra 100, 109, 111
types of 74, 75-7
yoga nidra 35, 77

ACKNOWLEDGMENTS

I have had the honor to meet and learn from so many great energy workers over the years. Their wisdom infuses every page of this book and I wholeheartedly thank them all—including Denise Linn, Sarah Shurety, Jane Mayers, Richard Lanham, Vera Diamond, Denise Leicester, Fiona Arrigo, Donna Lancaster, Gabi Krüger, Kim Bennett, Gertrud Keazor, Adele Nozedar, Zena Hallam, Caroline Shola Arewa, Amisha Ghadiali, Kate Taylor, Gail Love Schock, Tashidowa, Faraaz Tanveer, Mangalo Upasaka, Helga Himmelsbach, Gabrielle Roth, Jan Day, Dainei Tracy, Jonathan Goldman, Maurice and Nicola Griffin, Julian Baker, Gillie Gilbert, Maria Mercati, Jessica Loeb, Emma Field, Malcolm Kirsch, Theo Gimbel, Lynne Crawford, Sheila MacLeod, Marie-Louise Lacy, Harry Oldfield, Kenneth Meadows, Leo Rutherford, Ramses Seleem, Gina Lazenby, William Spear, Dr Rajendra Sharma, Doja Purkitt, Marilyn Glenville, Jane Thurnell-Read, Sue Weston, Andrew Chevalier, Karen Kingston, Will Parfitt, Dee Jones, Joel Carbonnel, Simon Brown, Paresh Rink, Margaret-Anne Pauffley and Paul Dennis, Allan Rudolf, Jennie Crewdson, Margareta Loughran, Kate Roddick, Serena Smith, Angela Renton, Susan Lever, Shan, Howard Charing, Dr Tamara Voronina, Pauline Groman, Nick Williams, Ben Renshaw, Pim de Gryff, Catherine Lewis McDougal, Barbara Ford Hammond, Jane Matthews, Anne-Marie Reed, Millie Ker, Donna Booth, Sebastian Pole, and Jeff Lennard.

Especial thanks to Margot Gordon, who planted the energy seed in my head, and to Belinda Budge, who first championed this book so many years ago. Adrian Tierney-Jones gave huge support on the home front.

Immense gratitude to the fabulous team at Kyle Books—Sophie Allen, Sarah Kyle, Caroline Alberti, Joanna Copestick, as well as Sarah Sutton and Annie Wilson. Designer Nicky Collings is responsible for making this book so beautiful and I am awestruck at the talent of Amalia Wahlström— her illustrations are all I dreamed of and way more.